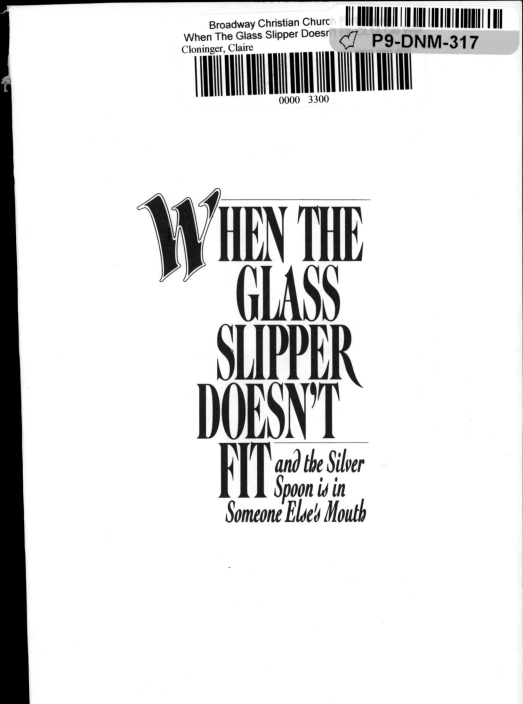

WHEN THE GLASS SLIPPER DOESN'T FIT *and the Silver Spoon is in Someone Else's Mouth*

Claire Cloninger
& Karla Worley

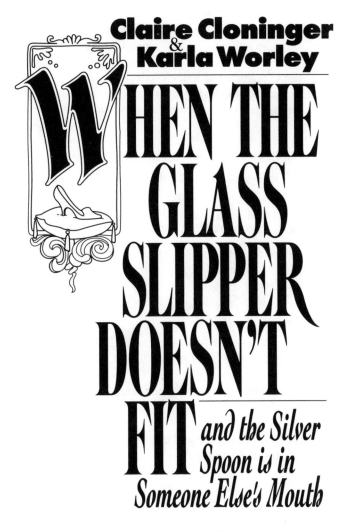

WHEN THE GLASS SLIPPER DOESN'T FIT *and the Silver Spoon is in Someone Else's Mouth*

WORD PUBLISHING
Dallas·London·Vancouver·Melbourne

WHEN THE GLASS SLIPPER DOESN'T FIT
AND THE SILVER SPOON IS IN SOMEBODY ELSE'S MOUTH:
On Surrendering Our Expectations and Celebrating Our Reality

Scripture quotations in this book are from the following versions:

The Living Bible (LB), copyright 1971 by Tyndale House Publishers, Wheaton, IL. Used by permission.

The New American Standard Bible (NASB), © The Lockman Foundation 1960, 1962, 1963, 1968, 1971, 1972, 1973, 1975, 1977.

The Holy Bible, New International Version® (NIV). Copyright © 1973, 1978, 1984 by International Bible Society. Used by permission of Zondervan Publishing House. All rights reserved.

The New King James Version (NKJV). Copyright © 1979, 1980, 1982, Thomas Nelson, Inc., Publisher.

The New Testament in Modern English (PHILLIPS) by J. B. Phillips, published by The Macmillan Company, © 1958, 1960, 1972 by J. B. Phillips.

Library of Congress Cataloging-in-Publication Data:

Cloninger, Claire.
    When the glass slipper doesn't fit and the silver spoon is in someone else mouth / Claire Cloninger, Karla Worley.
        p.   cm.
    ISBN 0–8499–3383–8 (pbk.)
        1. Women—Religious life.   2. Christian life—1960– .   I. Worley, Karla.   II. Title.
BV4527.C58   1993
248.8'43—dc20   93–21766
                                                                                          CIP

Printed in the United States of America

3 4 5 6 9   LB   9 8 7 6 5 4 3 2 1

To Virginia and Charlie, my Mom and Dad,
who always found a way
to make expectations seem possible
and reality seem bearable

Claire

To Dennis, Seth, Matt, and Ben,
whose presence in my life
is a constant reminder that
reality is the best fantasy of all

Karla

Contents

ONE

Up to My Elbows— And No Sign of a Prince

Karla's chapter about
things that just haven't turned out
the way they were supposed to

In the humdrum everydayness of our daily lives,
sometimes we rush right past amazing things,
like a flower bravely pushing through the sidewalk cracks,
or a robin on a phone wire that lifts his head and sings.

There are miracles around us,
though we are unaware.
While we wrestle lesser treasures
they are there,
whispering in our ear,
"Eternal things are here."
While we focus on each weary, waiting mile:
there are miracles around us all the while.

CLAIRE CLONINGER AND KARLA WORLEY[1]

I *spent most of* 1989 throwing up. I don't mean to be gross. But my second child, Matt, was born in November of that year. And for most of that time, I didn't feel like combing my hair, getting dressed, or doing much of anything but throwing up.

I was really looking forward to 1990; that was going to be the year I got my act together again. But I forgot what it's like to have a new baby. (God lets you forget . . . or else you might never have another one!) That was a long winter with long nights of very little sleep. By the time spring came, I had put on twenty-five pounds of postpartem weight and was feeling tired, fat, and generally miserable about myself. At a really low point, I wrote to my friend Claire:

> I am not Karla. I am a room mother; I am a backyard referee; I am the mean-old-mother-who-makes-Seth-practice-piano. I am the chauffeur, the cook, bottle-washer. I am the nursemaid; I am the accountant who pays the bills.
>
> Not to mention that I am supposed to have enough of me left to be friend, confidante, and colleague to my husband. And what tired, flabby, overworked, and grumpy woman feels like being romantic and sexy at the end of the day?
>
> I want to paint my nails. I want to go shopping. I want to curl up by the fire and read books. I want to sleep late. I want to have the energy to stay up late enough to see David Letterman. I don't want bags under my eyes. I don't want to buy industrial strength under-eye concealer. I don't want to shop in the "Woman's World" department; I want to shop in Juniors.
>
> I'd like to be the witty, sparkling conversationalist I once was; I want to be spontaneous. I want to be attractive and well-dressed. I don't even recognize this dumpy, grumpy person I see in the mirror.
>
> I feel like Cinderella must have felt, scrubbing baseboards and toting wood, knowing in her heart that she *could* be a princess . . . if only she had the dress, or the shoes, or the time to do her hair.
>
> Where's my fairy godmother? I could sure use that wand right now. I'd bop myself, my house, and my family with it, and *poof!* My life would finally fall into place.

Claire's boys are both grown and graduated. How I envied her long nights of uninterrupted sleep and her days full of freedom! But Claire, ever a wise friend, didn't rub it in. She wrote back with graciousness, sharing some of her own struggles with her writing career, with growing older, with readjusting to a move to the country and a suddenly empty nest. Although Claire was at a different stage in her life than I, she, too, was having trouble coming to grips with who she was. She wrote:

> I think the word I'm looking for is *surrender*. As in giving up. Not giving up our dreams of finally being allowed to be "Claire" and "Karla"; more like being willing to give up our *ideas* of who "Claire" and "Karla" really are.

I shared Claire's letter with some of my friends and discovered that they also shared these feelings of longing and frustration. All of us, at whatever stage in life we find ourselves, seem to feel that the realities of our lives just don't measure up. ("If I could take off that last ten pounds . . ." "If I could just do something with my hair . . ." "If I just had more time . . ." "If I had the money . . ." "I wish I were more talented . . .") And we'd all like to be something more than we are.

Let's face it, most of us grew up expecting to be Cinderella. We waited for the handsome prince, the fairy godmother, the horse-drawn carriage. When Princess Diana got married, we were all glued to the TV, fascinated with her because *she really got it*. (See, we knew all along it was possible!) Now we're finding out, as Diana did, that even the life of a princess is not all it's cracked up to be.

But most of us have had a moment, standing at our kitchen sinks elbow-deep in dishes, when we asked ourselves, "Hey! When's the guy with the glass slipper gonna show up so I can get out of here?" In our hearts, we're the princess; it's just that these ungrateful pumpkins and mice we live with don't seem to realize it.

I recently took my children to see Disney's movie *Cinderella* when it was rereleased in theaters. We had a great afternoon; we spilled popcorn and Coke, and my two-year-old ran up and down the aisles the whole time. And I had a great revelation. (Yes, it is possible to get a great revelation in a Disney movie filled with sticky preschoolers, spilled popcorn, and Coke all over the floor.)

Here it is: Cinderella was *happy*. And not just at the end of the story, when she had the glass slipper on her foot and the handsome Prince. Cinderella was happy at the beginning, slaving away for the wicked stepmother!

There she was, scrubbing the floor, and she was *singing*. Birds were twittering around her, the sun was shining just so on the sill, and Cinderella was ready to dance. I came out of the movie saying to myself, "I don't care about the glass slipper anymore; I want to know how she did *that!*"

Cinderella was as happy and lovely scrubbing floors as she was with a crown on her head. *That's* what made her a princess.

And though a fairy tale princess and a New Testament preacher might not seem to have much in common, the apostle Paul had something of the same outlook that Cinderella had. He put it this way: "I have learned how to get along happily whether I have much or little."[2] Those are words written from a prison cell. And in that unlikely place Paul, like Cinderella, found a reason to sing.

Suppose—just suppose—that you and I could learn to do that: to be happy in whatever state we find ourselves. To sing while we scrub floors. To ignore the wallpaper we can't afford to change and marvel at the way the sun shines on the windowsill. To love and forgive the flabby stomachs we got from having babies, the wrinkles we developed from smiling and crying. To see our children as miracles, our husbands as gifts, our jobs as opportunities. To look at pumpkins and see the possibilities. To stop waiting for the guy with the glass slipper. To rejoice in what we have today.

Wouldn't that be worth far more than a glass slipper? Wouldn't we really, then, be as rich as any princess with a kingdom all her own?

If you're one of those lucky people who can actually find time to read a book, then come with us on our journey. Hide out in the basement, send the kids to your neighbors, lock the bathroom door (or the office door) if you have to, but come with us. Pray with us. Ask God to show you how rich you are, what treasures you have, in whatever state you are. Ask him to teach you what Paul and Cinderella knew: that wherever you are, whatever you are doing, there is a reason you can sing.

Not that I speak from want;
for I have learned to be content
in whatever circumstances I am.
I know how to get along with humble means,
and I also know how to live in prosperity;
in any and every circumstance
I have learned the secret
of being filled and going hungry,
both of having abundance and suffering need.
I can do all things through Him who strengthens me.

PHILIPPIANS 4:11–13 NASB

What Are Your Circumstances?

As we begin our journey together,
jot down some answers
to these three questions:

(1) What did I expect for my life
(my hopes and dreams?)
(2) What am I still hoping for?
(3) What circumstances in my life
are reason to rejoice?

Lord, help me to learn to adopt Paul's attitude,
to be happy in whatever circumstances I find myself.
Help me to surrender my fantasies,
my castles in the air.
Help me to see what is good about my life
and to have a thankful heart.
Lord, give me a song, and help me to sing.

AMEN

TWO

Moving to Disney World Is Not an Option

Claire's chapter about signing a peace treaty with reality

Accepting what I can't change, changing what I can,
going with God's power, flowing with his plan—
the less I push and struggle, the freer I will be,
and my song will be "sweet serenity."

Oh, serenity, sweet serenity—
there's a Love that's higher reaching down to me.
Oh, serenity, sweet serenity—
there's a Hope that's deeper than the depths of me.
Oh, serenity,
sweet serenity.

Trusting and believing, one day at a time,
reaching out and sharing all the love I find—
the more I give to others, the more there is for me,
and my song will be "sweet serenity."

CLAIRE CLONINGER AND LYNN KEESECKER[1]

I *will never forget* my first visit to Disney World—that wonderful place where reality is temporarily suspended and everything seems possible. For me, it felt very much like coming home. I kept thinking to myself, "This is where I belong—it's where I've always belonged."

I gasped when I first glimpsed the shimmering towers of Cinderella's castle rising before me. Starry-eyed, I turned to to my husband, Spike and said, "Oh, it's so beautiful. I just wish we could *live* right here in Fantasyland."

Spike never missed a beat.

"Claire," he said gently, "You've been living in fantasyland ever since I met you."

Spike has this amazing way of bringing me right back down to earth. And I need that, because dealing with life realistically has never been my strong suit. I would describe my general approach to life as "whimsical" rather than "practical"—as "imaginative" rather than "down-to-earth." (Other people who have had the pleasure of living with me might be more inclined to call me "clueless" or even "out to lunch.")

Reality, in all of its blacks and whites, has always been a struggle for me. I mean it's just so . . . so real. But unfortunately, as I have had to learn, there are no "for sale" signs on the colorful streets of Disney World; nobody is moving in on a permanent basis. At some point, every one of its visitors packs up, heads home, and settles down to something called real life.

Real life means "what is" and not what we had envisioned or hoped for. It means leaving the castles in the clouds and climbing down the beanstalk to planet earth. It means making a peace treaty between our expectations and our reality.

And therein lies the rub. For I came to the conclusion a long time ago that discontent is almost always linked to expectations. For most of us the problem is not what we get in life but what we get that's different from what we expected.

GREAT EXPECTATIONS—AND REAL OUTCOMES

If we could enter kindergarten or college or marriage or motherhood with absolutely no expectations, we'd probably be spared a lot of grief. Or better yet, if someone could just give us an accurate summary of what to expect from any of the above, we might at least be prepared.

Instead, all too often we find ourselves embarking on our most important life journeys with inaccurate and misleading road maps. They are maps we've been forced to draw for ourselves based on things like childhood hearsay, cultural myths, and media hype.

For instance, think back on your expectations of romance. Where did they come from? My romantic expectations were shaped by several forces, most significantly Doris Day movies. In these movies, Doris behaved in a coy, madcap, and basically air-headed manner for two solid hours as she subtly but relentlessly pursued Rock Hudson or some reasonable facsimile of him. She manipulated like mad and even lied shamelessly at times. But never mind. Rock (or whoever) eventually found himself hopelessly smitten with her anyway and all ended happily. So what was I to assume?

Other influences that shaped my romantic expectations were (1) spying on my sister, Alix, when her boyfriends came over; (2) listening, fascinated, for hours to my next-door-neighbor, Carolyn, who was one year older and purported to know absolutely everything about boys; and, of course, (3) the mysterious appearance of certain Ann Landers columns, offering advice to the young and lovelorn, which I would find neatly clipped from the daily paper and attached with a clothespin to my lampshade.

From that motley mixture of advice and innuendo, I fashioned my expectations of romance. So how closely did the reality of love and romance match my youthful expectations? Go figure.

I also had faulty and inaccurate expectations in other areas of my life—college, adulthood, and motherhood, to name a few. From my personal experience with expectations I have formulated a sort of general-purpose hypothesis which goes something like this: "What we expect in life and what really happens don't necessarily have all that much in common."

Random data in support of my hypothesis can be found in almost anybody's life—notably yours and mine. For instance,

- We expected a Barbie doll from Aunt Sally for Christmas, and instead we got a Baby Wets-a-lot.

- We expected sunshine the day of the picnic, and instead we got rain (also ants).

- We expected Mr. Wonderful to ask us to the prom, and instead we got a call from the president of Nerds Anonymous.

- We expected our husbands to be a perfect combination of our fathers and Cary Grant (or Paul Newman or Mel Gibson), and they had the audacity to be themselves.

- We expected a glamorous and exciting career, and instead we got eight hours behind a desk and a forty-five-minute commute.

- We expected life to be logical and manageable and somehow "fair." And it turned out to be, at times, about as manageable as a room full of rattlesnakes and about as logical as an adolescent in love.

Now, there is no possible way for me to see the gulf which lies between your expectations and your reality. Perhaps life has handed you everything you've ever dreamed of on a silver platter. Perhaps you were born beautiful and brilliant and gifted and popular with just exactly the right-sized foot to glide gracefully into the glass slipper (which of course was held out to you on a satin cushion by a dashingly handsome prince). Perhaps the silver spoon which has been in your mouth since birth has multiplied into a complete place setting for twelve.

But why do I suspect that the above scenario is not an accurate description of your life? In the first place, I've never met anyone whose life could be summed up that beautifully. In the second place, would you even have reached for this book if the glass slipper was already comfortably on your foot and the silver spoon was already clenched firmly between your evenly spaced, cavity-free teeth?

No, I have a hunch that you, like the rest of us, have already had at least some experience with life's occasional habit of dream dashing and expectation crunching. (My sister summed it up pretty well after her divorce when she said, "It's not just the man and the marriage I'm grieving for; it's this crazy dream I've always had that everything would turn out 'happily-ever-after.'")

I'm not trying to be morbid or morose or anything. It's just that real lives are not anything at all like fairy-tale lives. Even I have managed to learn that. And if you're anywhere past puberty, I have a sneaking suspicion you've already skinned your knee on reality at least once or twice by now. If you haven't, you will. My mom, who is not only the mother of five but also a psychologist and something of a sage, puts it this way: "If you're not struggling with something right now, line up! It'll be your turn soon."

SKUBALON HAPPENS

So here's another conclusion I have come to after lo, these many years: "Real life" or "reality" is what actually happens while you're waiting around for your expectations to pan out the way you thought they should.

I heard a wonderful sermon once about reality and its total disregard for our expectations. The Reverend Marshall P. Craver III entitled his message "Skubalon Happens." Inspired by a certain tasteless bumper sticker, he had looked up the Greek word for "dung," which he found to be *skubalon*. His sermon was an inspired message on the redemptive power of God when life's unexpected, unplanned-for unpleasantries conspire to derail our best-laid plans.

Jesus never pulled any punches about "reality." He never set out any false expectations. He told his followers in the clearest possible terms that in this world they would most definitely run head-on into tribulation—trouble, trials, yea, even "skubalon."

"But be of good cheer," he continued, "I have overcome the world."[2]

Of course, Jesus' ultimate victory over real life on this earth lies in his power to see us through it and finally lift us out of it after death. The plane and quality of eternal existence which we are promised with him at that point is Real in the capital-letter sense. But he made it very clear that his power is for the here and now, also.

So he seems to be saying, "Yes, you do have to live in the real world. And I know that it's no picnic. See, I lived here, too. But don't let it do you in. In me, there *is* a way of overcoming. You can't live in Fantasyland, but you don't have to wallow in the *skubalon*, either!

Stick with me. Trust me. And I'll give you what you need to live victorious lives in the real world."

WELCOME TO THE REAL WORLD

But just exactly what do I mean by living in "the real world"? Essentially, living in the real world means coping with the nitty-gritty and the everyday. Waking up. Brushing our teeth. Feeding the dog, the parakeet, the family (whatever). Getting dressed and going about the business of doing whatever it is we do to exist on planet earth.

And, yes, everybody has to do it.

Reality means going to work—or staying home to work, or not being able to find work. It means paying the bills and cooking a meal and sometimes feeling trapped or lonely or scared or unappreciated.

It means nurturing our relationships, or working hard on difficult relationships, or sometimes being forced to watch a treasured relationship die, however hard we may have tried to save it. It means allowing the people we love to make their own choices and mistakes, just as we must make our own.

It means using every scrap of our grit, our wit, and our God-given imagination to make the very best we can out of the actual-fact existence we've been given—good days, bad days, and in-between days.

And living in reality, coping with real life in the real world, is one of the biggest challenges of being human. The extent to which we are able to pull it off with some measure of serenity, grace, and purpose will, to a great degree, determine the quality of our existence.

The way I've observed it, there are three main ways that people deal with the down side of reality. Each has something to recommend it, but each falls short as a full-time strategy for handling life. Take it from me. I know. I've tried every one of them!

Strategy # 1: "Don't Look at It and Maybe It Will Go Away"

Denial has become a popular buzzword of our generation, primarily because so many of us are into it. I myself have learned a lot about denial by spending a considerable amount of time doing it on different occasions. I have learned during my seasons of denial what it is and what it is not. And as the now-famous T-shirt says, denial is definitely not "a river in Egypt."

Denial means, essentially, in the words of the old musical, "closing your eyes to a situation you do not wish to acknowledge." It's a trick your mind can pull when you really don't want to face some aspect of reality; it simply arranges to blind you to the fact that the reality exists. It's there, but you just can't see it.

Denial in its place is appropriate. It is said to be one of the initial stages of grief and an indispensable step on the journey to wholeness after a loss. It gives you time to absorb the reality of the loss gradually.

Denial in response to loss is similar to what happens when the body goes into shock after a trauma. Normal physical functions slow down temporarily in order to give the body time to recover its equilibrium. It's the body's way of shutting down so that we won't bleed to death or go into a total panic. But if a person remains in shock without being "brought back," the shock itself can prove harmful, even fatal.

I experienced some healthy and appropriate denial during the time that I grieved the death of Spike's mother, Marjorie, who was my close friend. It took me more than a year after her death to absorb the fact that she was actually gone. Over and over, I would pick up the phone to call her, or I'd remind myself to tell her something funny that had happened. Only gradually did my mind adjust to the reality that she was gone.

Short of developing a psychosis, however, there was no way I could *permanently* deny the reality of Marjorie's death. Even though, deep inside, I had somehow expected that she would always be there for me, I eventually had to come out of that stage of denial and finally face the reality that she was not.

Even though denial can be helpful and even life-saving under certain circumstances, refusing to let go of our denial can be very unhealthy and even deadly. The storm we refuse to prepare for can sink our ship. The physical symptoms we choose to ignore can become a full-blown, incurable disease. The rift in a relationship can become a crack, then a canyon, and finally a divorce. Clinging blindly and stubbornly to our expectations and refusing to see the reality of what is really happening cuts us off from the truth and its power to free us.

Mae West, the early film star, had one of the most classic cases of denial I've ever heard of. She was very beautiful and glamorous in her younger days, and I suppose she expected that her glamor would never fade. As the inevitable wrinkles and lines began to mar her famous face, it is said that Mae West had all of the mirrors removed from her home. If she didn't have to look into the face of reality, she could live on in the land of her unreality.

My great-uncle Ferdinand, too, was a man of stubborn expectations undergirded by denial, or so the family story goes. Ferdinand was the patriarch of a large Roman Catholic family, and it was his heart's desire that one of his sons would go into the priesthood.

Of each son, as he came along, Uncle Ferdinand would say in his French accent, "Wonderful boy! Bright as a silver dollar! He's going to be a priest!" None of his sons, however, was even remotely interested in going into the ministry, and none of them ever did.

I can't help but wonder how much time my great-uncle wasted in clinging to his expectations rather than getting to know his boys' own real hopes and ambitions.

Like Uncle Ferdinand, I had expectations for my own two boys. I don't remember specifically putting them into words, but I'm sure my children heard and "felt" those expectations a million different ways. I expected my children to do well and to live up to their academic potential. I expected them to grow up to be nice, polite people and to fit easily into our lives.

Some of my most dramatic lessons in getting past denial have been coming to understand that children arrive with their own personalities and styles of doing things. They come with their own temperaments and quickly develop their own agendas. And they don't always fit in with what we had in mind.

Both of our sons are total originals! Curt, our oldest, from earliest childhood was very verbal and inquisitive, with a thoroughly unique way of viewing life. He took nothing for granted and questioned everything.

But it was our younger son, Andy's, impulsiveness and risk-taking that set me on a journey of deadly denial. What had been adventuresome and mischievous in grade school became dangerous and destructive in high school. Gradually, between grades nine and ten, we watched Andy's grades drop, his friendships change, his attitudes and behavior change. Every warning sign possible for teenage alcohol and drug abuse was blinking in my face, and yet I didn't see what was happening.

The fact is, I wouldn't see it. I couldn't. Everything in me was working overtime to tell me that Andy's behavior did not indicate what I secretly feared must surely be. And because I lived in this state of denial for months and years, our family got sicker instead of healthier, and we almost lost our son.

The good news is that I did get better. Our whole family did. But this improvement was not an overnight thing. On my way to getting better, I moved from a state of denying that the problem existed to another way of dealing with reality. I moved into the "fix it" mode.

Strategy #2: "If It's Broke, Fix It!"

The "fix it" mode has much to recommend it as a means of dealing with real life problems. A lot of things *can* be fixed, helped, polished, and generally improved by our own efforts. Nothing makes us feel better than to fix something up.

My mom, in her practice of psychology, often counsels with people who feel that their lives are totally out of control. And sometimes she gives a simple and surprising initial assignment to these "chaotic" types: Clean up your car! She actually sends them off, instructing them not to return until they have done a really super job on the interior and the exterior of their automobiles—dejunking, washing, polishing, the works! It's surprising how often these people will come back thoroughly revived and ready to take on the rest of their problems after having had that one, small success at getting something in shape.

But there's a problem with the fix-it approach: it can become an addictive way of life. People can get stuck there. And I should know.

People who get stuck in the "fix it" mode are sometimes called "fixers." They are people who shop in the "self-help" section of their local bookstores. I know that, too, because I see them there.

Which reminds me of a long-ago incident that tipped me off to my "fix it" addiction. One of our favorite babysitters back in the days when our children were little was a delightful, sandy-haired teen named Andolyn. Andolyn possessed the refreshing but sometimes unsettling ability to assess a situation and "tell it like it is."

One evening after getting our boys to bed, Andolyn decided to browse through my bedroom bookshelf. And there she discovered my secret passion for self-help books!

"Mama," she told her mother (who is my friend), the next day, "either Mrs. Cloninger knows a whole lot about 'how to' do almost everything, or she is in big trouble!"

In my private stash of reading materials, Andolyn had discovered how-to books on every subject from decorating to dieting, from macramé to microwaves, from resume writing to river rafting. Digging through the stacks, she also found archeological evidence of my pop psychology days, including books that encouraged me to be my own best friend, to pull my own strings, to convince myself that I was okay and you were, too, to locate my erroneous personality zones, and to treat my psyche cybernetically.

If there were a twelve-step recovery program for "fixers," I would long ago have had to confess to the group, "My name is Claire, and I am a recovering self-help junkie!"

The problem with being a self-help-addicted fixer is not immediately apparent to the fixer herself because, like other addictions, this problem accelerates gradually. We have one small success, and we think we can fix anything and everything. We start with automobile interiors, and the next thing we know we are trying to overhaul our bosses, our husbands, our children, and the entire membership of our churches. We change a tire or a hairdo or the wallpaper in the breakfast room, and the next thing we know we wrongly assume that we also have the power to change and control any and all of those "real life" circumstances which ooze outside the boundaries of our expectations.

The key lesson in the life of any fixer is learning what can be fixed by our efforts and what cannot. What can be bulldozed or restructured or redone by the sweat of our brow and the determination of our spirits, and what must be surrendered and accepted. It is learning what part prayer and faith can play in making changes, and at what point we have stopped praying and started nagging—stopped seeking God's will and started using our prayers to bully God into doing our will.

A fixer has to learn when "fixing" helps and when it hurts. For instance, what is appropriate in reorganizing a dresser drawer is usually inappropriate, ineffective, and counterproductive when applied to reorganizing the lives of other human beings.

The single most difficult lesson I have learned in my life as a recovering fixer has been coming to the realization that I cannot change or fix other people. Not even if I feel that I know what is best for them. Not even if I see them destroying themselves and I feel that they must be stopped. Not even if I love them desperately and only want to help. I cannot fix other people. I have learned that to try to do so is to thwart that other person's emotional and spiritual growth. To try to change another person is one of the best ways in the world to destroy my relationship with that person. I can pray and love and encourage. But I cannot change anyone else.

I am learning, too, that I cannot reconstruct or orchestrate or manipulate every "real life" event that comes along to upset my best-laid plans. I cannot make life turn out the way I expected just by an act of my will.

Manipulating and refashioning reality is God's job. He is good at it. He knows what he's trying to accomplish and I don't. Most of us fixers have a secret suspicion that we could do a better job than God if he'd only move over and give us a shot. But we are totally wrong about that. Most of us fixers must eventually face the very difficult task of getting out of the God business and making room for the only One who knows how to do it right.

When I finally let go of my denial and admitted that my precious younger son was in the grips of an alcohol and drug addiction, I unconsciously assumed it was my job to fix him. I thought if I could just pray a little harder, love him a little more fervently, be a little bit better mother, I could lift him out of the deep and dangerous hole he had dug for himself.

I thought that if I bought him clothes that made him look like a model teenager I could make him into a model teenager. I thought that if I would stay up typing his term papers, I could pull him out of the fire scholastically. I thought that I could coax him or reason him or shame him or love him into changing his life. And I just about killed myself trying.

What I found out was that my efforts to save him were driving the nails into his coffin. As long as I was owning his problem, he would never own it. As long as I was staying up nights trying to fix his life, he could get a good night's sleep and wake up rested and ready to rebel a little harder the next day.

I had worried and paced and prayed myself into a state of exhausted insanity. My prayers were everything but faithful petitions; I was threatening and whining and begging and nagging before the throne of grace.

"God, make him change. You've got to make him change," I kept saying.

And it wasn't happening.

At that point, my friend Rita, who had gone through a similar problem, began to share her experience, strength, and hope with me. Through her example, I began to understand that my prayers and my faith and my Christian walk had to change. I could see that Rita's son only began to get well emotionally when she became willing to let go of him and his problem. When he finally realized she was no longer trying to fix him, he began to deal with his own problems and get well himself.

The Lord showed me through Rita and her life that I had to begin to let go. I had to stop trying to be God in Andy's life and let God do his job. I had to begin to deal with my own sick spirit and stop focusing all of my energy on Andy. Only in this way would he be able to own his problem and begin to deal with it.

When a fixer is finally ready to stop fixing, she's ready to get well. When a fixer is finally ready to stop trying to be God, she is ready to move to the next method of dealing with reality—acceptance.

Strategy #3: "That's the Way It Is"

I realize that acceptance is not the total answer. Obviously, accepting anything and everything would be foolish and fatalistic. It would leave us with no hope and preempt our faith.

But learning to recognize and accept the things we cannot change is one of the most vital steps to be taken in dealing with real life and its dilemmas. This kind of acceptance is a power position because it finally puts us in touch with things as they are. It puts us in touch with, and helps us make peace with, the truth. And like the Bible says, that will set you free!

I remember reading the testimony of a woman (I'll call her Karen) and her struggle to accept herself. Karen had been overweight since her teens, and she hated her body. She also blamed and shamed herself over and over for her inability to change her eating habits and lose weight.

Every winter, Karen would determine to lose weight before the next summer. How she longed to lie on the beach, which was only a few miles from her home town. How she longed to walk in the waves and feel the wind in her hair the way she had as a child. Every year she would begin by taking off twenty pounds (about half of what she needed to lose). But every year, by the time summer arrived, she had begun to put it on again.

One summer day, as she looked in the mirror and faced her failure once more, Karen realized how much she hated herself. She realized, too, that by clinging to her self-hatred, she was actually giving herself a prison sentence.

"You may not go to the beach until you are perfect, Karen," she was telling herself. As she realized the cruelty and unacceptance she had held in her heart toward herself, Karen wept.

"Would I lock any other overweight person up and forbid them to go to the beach?" she asked herself. She knew that she would not. She would love and encourage anyone else in her position. But instead of showing that kind of love and encouragement to herself, she had become her very own "wicked stepmother," condemning herself to a sad, isolated life.

"Father, forgive me," Karen prayed. "Forgive me for my cruelty to myself. You love me even though I am overweight. You look at me and give me kindness and forgiveness and grace and encouragement. But I have been giving myself only condemnation and cruelty. Help me, Father, to accept and love myself as I am."

An overwhelming tenderness filled Karen's heart at that moment. She knew that what she was experiencing was the tender love of her heavenly Father. She stood before the mirror and looked at herself. What she saw there was a lovely, dark-haired, gentle, overweight woman, with tears streaming down her face, who had not been to the beach in twenty-two years!

At that moment, Karen determined to begin accepting herself. She decided to be on her own side instead of always being her own worst enemy. Karen went shopping that weekend and bought a black swimsuit with hot-pink stripes, a matching beach coat, and hot-pink flip-flops. Then, on impulse, she went into the children's department and bought a plastic bucket and shovel. Now she was ready!

That very afternoon, Karen drove to the beach alone. She kept reminding herself of God's love and acceptance. As Karen stepped into the sand and kicked off her new flip-flops, she re-experienced that old childhood pleasure of sand between her toes.

Karen looked into the faces of the people as she walked by them down the beach. At one time she would have imagined that they were sneering or laughing cruelly at her. Now she knew that the cruel laughter had been in her mind. The people walking by simply saw an overweight woman in a large-size black bathing suit who was obviously taking pleasure in the sunshine and the waves.

The irony of accepting an unpleasant "reality" in our lives is that acceptance often opens a door to change. It was only when Karen was willing to accept and love herself as she was, extra pounds and all, that she was finally able to begin changing her behavior and her appearance.

A GRADUAL HEALING

As I accepted the reality of Andy's addiction, and (by far the hardest step) let go of the idea that I could fix him, I began to find a new level of peace in my own life. Though the situation did not improve right away, I began to see the dynamics of our family system in a way that I had never seen it before. Like the little child in "The Emperor's New Clothes," I could see what was what!

I began to be able to pray aright again, to put Andy in God's hands and leave him there. And my husband Spike and I began to pray together in a new and special way—that God would bring some consequences to Andy's behavior which would create a crisis in his life and show him his need for help. It was a scary prayer to pray, but we knew that our son would never ask for or accept help until he could see the need with his own eyes.

During this time, we began concentrating on what we could do something about: our own problems—for example, our denial, our anger, and our control needs. Though our child's problem was getting worse, we began to get better. We were growing closer as a couple and becoming more at peace as individuals.

Our special prayers for Andy were answered one August night shortly after his graduation from high school. He was arrested and jailed for buying liquor with a forged driver's license. The charge was second-degree forgery, a felony offense. At one time, this would have seemed like a tremendous tragedy, but both Spike and I immediately recognized it as God's hand operating in our situation.

We decided not to rush right in to rescue Andy when he called, as we once might have done. Instead we let him spend the night in a crowded, depressing cell of the Mobile City Jail, locked in with five other drug offenders. During that long, sobering night, Andy could feel God "knocking on his door."

The very next week, at a Christian mountain-climbing camp, Andy gave his life to the Lord. He came home from camp with a new faith and a new determination to change with God's help. It was Andy's own decision to enter a ten-week rehabilitation program where he could learn some badly needed skills for living sober.

PEACE BETWEEN "WHAT YOU WANTED" AND "WHAT YOU GOT"

Andy was not the only one who learned a lot during his time in rehab. Spike and I drove over to the treatment center every Saturday to watch films and hear lectures on this disease of addiction. Our older son, Curt, took a week off from college to go through "family week" with us.

It was during this challenging time that we discovered the power of praying the well-known Serenity Prayer. We found it to be a prayer which leads out of denial, past the fix-it urge, and beyond fatalistic acceptance. It helps us see things realistically, thereby allowing us to determine the difference between what we can fix and what we must accept.

During the difficult, exhausting, amazing, miracle-filled weeks that Andy was in treatment, I learned to pray this famous prayer with a whole new sense of understanding. Every day I would pray it in this way:

God, grant me the serenity to accept the things I cannot change . . . I cannot change Andy or his addiction. I cannot make him live sober or walk with the Lord. I cannot control the situations which he will encounter when he gets out of treatment. I cannot single-handedly overhaul this culture in which we live—a culture which offers dangerous, life-threatening options to our children. Grant me the serenity to accept the things I cannot change.

Grant me the courage to change the things I can change . . . Lord, I am the only person I can change. I can learn to trust and love and let go of fear. I can learn to encourage others without demanding them to be what I think they should. I can work on my own problems and weaknesses and hang-ups. I can pray with real power and faith and release and abandon, surrendering my worry to your strength. I can share my experience, strength, and hope with other parents who are going through what I went through. I can make my home a place of welcome and refuge for my family. Grant me the courage to make these changes.

And Lord, grant me the wisdom to know the difference between the things which must be accepted and the things which can be changed. This kind of wisdom can only come from you, Lord. Amen.

Real life in the real world is a tough, nitty-gritty journey that every pilgrim on planet earth must make. Moving to Disney World is not an option. There will be tribulation; Jesus said so. But be of good cheer. He's still in the business of guiding and strengthening and healing and overcoming. And there really is serenity for the asking, right in the middle of it all. And, at the end, Real Life with him forever.

A POSTSCRIPT

The last three and a half years we have watched our son struggle and keep believing and praying and growing stronger. We have marveled at the growth and maturity he is finding in the Lord—all by himself, without his mama to fix it for him! Just last month, all of us had to sit back amazed at how God is able to overcome the downward pull of real life on planet earth. We celebrated Andy's acceptance of a brand-new job as youth pastor of our church!

Now listen, you who say,
"Today or tomorrow we will go
to this or that city, spend a year there,
carry on business and make money."
Why, you do not even know what will happen tomorrow.
What is your life?
You are a mist that appears for a little while
and then vanishes."

JAMES 4:13, 14 NIV

No eye has seen,
no ear has heard,
no mind has conceived
what God has prepared for those who love him.

1 CORINTHIANS 2:9 NIV

Embrace Real Life

Think of one major aspect of your life
where reality has fallen outside the boundaries of your
expectations. Describe it in writing.
Are you still struggling with this problem?
Ask God to give you his insight into it.
Then, using Claire's version of the Serenity Prayer
as a model, write out your present understanding
of what can be changed and what must be accepted
in your situation. (Be specific!)
Ask God for his peace and the courage and
wisdom to do what must be done.
Go to lunch or coffee with your closest friend
and share your insights with her.

Lord, thank you for the reality of my life—
just as it is today. Thank you for the grace
and the guidance you've given me
to go through what I've been through already.
Lord, I know I've let you and myself and other people
down at times. Forgive me.
Grant me a new perspective on my life . . . a new beginning.
And even as I am learning to live with joy in this one
moment, give me a glimpse of the beautiful things
you hold in store for me in this life and
in your ultimate kingdom of Reality.
Help me learn, with your grace, to live my life today
with joy and celebration for who I am in you.

AMEN

THREE

Mirror, Mirror
On the Wall

Karla's chapter about
not being an Ideal Woman
(but not being an
ugly stepsister, either)

Little toes,
you have already walked across my soul.

For nine long months,
you left your imprint on the inside of me,
where no one else could see.

Now you press them, pink and curled,
on the outside of my world,
where everyone can see them
as I've seen them from the start:

the tiny, wrinkled footprints of God
upon my heart.

KARLA WORLEY[1]

It happened to me just the other day, at Wal-Mart. It was just an average summer day. I was there with two of my boys, shopping for flip-flops, pool toys, and sunscreen. Then I stopped to look at the swimsuit cover-ups, and the entire fashion industry insulted me, right to my face.

It was a white T-shirt cover-up with a sailboat on the front, hanging on a rack on the women's clothing aisle, looking perfectly harmless. Then I looked for my size, and I read the tag: "One Size Fits Most."

Most? One size fits *most?* To me, it was quite obvious what they were saying: *"Most people would fit in this. How about you?"*

Well, maybe it would have fit me. But I'll never know, because I was not about to try it on. I walked away and left it hanging there, like a reproach.

IN QUEST OF THE IDEAL WOMAN

Why is our self-image so tied up in the physical? Well, maybe yours isn't. . . . But there have been times in my life when I could have flown a spaceship to Mars, become the first woman President, and won a Nobel prize, yet would still have felt like a failure if my skirt wouldn't zip up.

I bet I've been on just about every diet available. I've eaten all protein, eaten all carbohydrates, eaten all fruit, eaten nothing. I've jogged, walked, aerobicized, jazz-danced, low-impacted. Four different sizes of clothes hang in my closet, each representing a different stage of success or failure at living up to the Ideal.

And what is that Ideal? There is a multi-mega-million-dollar fashion industry out there devoted to promoting it—shaping our image of the Ideal body, the Ideal clothes, the Ideal hair, the Ideal face—the Ideal everything.

The Ideal Woman never ages. She has ten perfectly manicured nails, the sleek body of a sixteen-year-old, hair that never frizzes or goes limp, lipstick that stays in place, lashes that "never clump or flake." She looks equally good in her satin teddy as she does in her executive silk suit. I would hate her if she lived next door to me, but I must confess that, more than once, I have tried to *become* her.

And I have never succeeded.

The reality is, I've had three children. I have stretch marks—and my stomach was never that flat before I had children. (In fact, one of my favorite things about pregnancy is that for nine whole months, you don't have to hold your stomach in!)

I inherited my mother's Horrible Hair, which has the consistency of a broom (no offense, Mom). I have crow's feet around my eyes, and just the other day I discovered a big wrinkle—more like a crease—developing on my forehead. (I think that if you're starting to get wrinkles, you shouldn't have to have pimples anymore. Fair is fair.)

No, I'm afraid Ideal is out of reach for me, as it is for most of us. Now, I know there really are some Ideal Women out there, because I run into one every now and then at the mall. (Of course, she's shopping in a different department than I am!) I look at her, and I do not think, "Wow, she must be exhausted." But, in fact, she really must be. It takes a lot of work to be Ideal. It's a constant vigil. A perpetual watch for hangnails, gray hairs, dry skin, and that great enemy of all Ideal Women: cellulite.

Here is one reason I'm not Ideal: I don't have the time. I sit down to tweeze my eyebrows, and somebody can't find their socks. I couldn't give myself a facial, because there'd be a phone call and I'd have to go pick somebody up from soccer practice with green mud on my face.

All my life, I have wanted to have beautiful fingernails. My cousin Marcy had gorgeous, long, slender fingers and beautiful nails, even when we were in grade school. I have stubby, pawlike hands and nails that are usually peeled off to the quick. And yet I spent the greater part of my youth in quest of Ideal nails. In high school, my friend Kathy and I used her Dad's commercial-grade super-glue to attach false nails; we could have hung by them from the Empire State Building!

But I've come to accept that Ideal nails are not for me. I can't seem to grow them, and I can't afford the time or money for the upkeep on sculptured nails. My short, craggy nails are just more practical. And so I've developed a sort of secret prejudice against women who have long nails. I suspect they must also have a maid, because I know they can't do dishes or scrub bathtubs with those elegant hands. At the least, someone must follow them around to button up their blouses and pop open the tabs on their Coke cans! (I may not have gorgeous hands, but boy, can I open a Coke!)

Now, I'm not advocating neglecting our appearance. I'm just talking about getting some reality in our perspective. I want to look my best, but not at the expense of more important things in my life. And that means I need to learn to lighten up about my body, or my nails, or whatever it is that bothers me about the way I look.

After all, do I really want to be Ideal if it means my children can't hug me because they might mess up my hair? And is the Ideal wardrobe all that great if it means I can't get down and roll in the grass a little? (So what if I get grass stains on my rear. I can always "Shout it out"!)

Sometimes you simply have to let go of the Ideal in favor of the Truly Important. And most of the time I'm okay with that. I discovered with my first son, Seth, that silk blouses were completely impractical for a young mother. I used to go into my closet and pray to find something without spit on the shoulder! We'd go out to lunch on Sunday, and I'd spend my time dodging little fistfuls of red Jell-O. Before very long, silk went into the attic.

After a while, I got the blouses out again, safely. Then Matt came along, and I'm temporarily back to wash-n-wear. Silk is gorgeous, but it's just not worth the worry. I wouldn't want to miss one sticky little hug that comes my way. There'll be plenty of years ahead to wear silk (until my grandchildren come along!).

THE BODY OF CHRIST

Christ was not afraid to be mussed or sullied. He didn't worry about sweating or getting dirty. In fact, he did manual labor, which means he probably got seriously grubby at times. He was a King, but nobody waited on him; in fact, he waited on others. He washed feet. He served meals. He touched and hugged, laughed and wept, and I'll bet he sat on the floor.

He gave us an example: "This is my body, which is broken for you."[2] And Paul tells us in his writing that in this present world, we really are the body of Christ.

Now, I know that Paul used that phrase to talk about unity in diversity, but he was talking about our physical reality, too. Our physical bodies—however lumpy or short-limbed or skinny or pale—are Christ's tools for doing his work in this world. My pastor, Mike Glenn, often closes our service by reminding us, "If Jesus is to touch anyone this week, it will be with your hands. If he goes anywhere, it will be on your feet. You are the body of Christ."

As Christ's body, I can do some wonderful things. I can touch. I can hug. I can give a drink of water. I can bandage a skinned knee. I can laugh and splash in the creek. I can yell my head off at a soccer game or silently speak volumes, looking into my husband's eyes by candlelight. I can bake bread. I can bear children. I can read to them and rock them. I can share the pain of their disappointments, celebrate their victories, listen to their confidences, kiss away their hurts. I can be a listening ear for a friend, a shoulder to lean on. I am fearfully and wonderfully made.

And so are you! Short or tall, skinny or not so skinny, single or married, young or old . . . your body is much more than just a pair of breasts, a womb, a flat stomach, or a great complexion. Your particular combination of arms, ears, eyes, hands, feet, a heart—added to your own set of gifts and opportunities—make your experience of being human as unique to you as mine is to me. Contrary to what the media shows us and tells us, there is no standard for femininity. Part of the miracle of being a woman is that each of us, like a snowflake, is a complete and completely original expression of womanhood. And with each day that goes by, we are constantly changing and expressing in a new and different way the person we are.

Bob Benson, author and father, used to tell a great story about his son, who said that he was really jealous of his younger, toddler-aged brother. Bob asked him why. "Because," said the boy, "he has all them new things."

I feel the same envy as I watch my son discover "all them new things." Everything is wondrous! Look, Mommy, I can walk. Look, Mommy, I can put on my coat. Look, Mommy, I can pet the kitty. (Look, Mommy, I can stuff him in my toybox!) Life is a celebration to Matt. He is celebrating himself. And the song of his celebration is "Look at me!"

I know that I must regain this childlike view of myself, or I will waste the years with a bunch of "if onlys."

"If only" is the most futile phrase in the English language. It is not my friend. It does not help me deal with reality; it just leads me to build more Cinderella castles of fantasy . . . castles in the air.

THE ME I SEE

In his book, *Money, Sex, and Power,* Richard Foster writes that the reason pornography is so destructive is that it corrupts our ability to appreciate reality. No average housewife, reasons Foster, can compete with an airbrushed centerfold. The centerfold is fantasy; nobody really looks like that. But the more time a man spends with this fantasy, the less reality appeals to him.

In a subtle way, the fashion magazines and media have offered us their own version of pornography: slim, sleek bodies of eighteen-year-olds made up to look thirty. This, we have been told, is the Ideal. This is how a woman should look. But this high-fashion Ideal is just as much a fantasy as the centerfold. Most of us will never be able to look like that.

In fact, most models say it takes hours of makeup and hairstyling and a lifetime of rigorous diet and exercise in order for *them* to look like that. But most of us have fifteen minutes to put on our makeup. We don't have personal trainers or people to follow us around with special lighting. So what's our realistic hope of ever measuring up?

Our culture is doing a number on us, and it's hard to escape it. Psychologists tell us that until girls reach the age of ten or eleven, they are fairly self-confident and have a positive body image. But only two years later, they have developed a negative body image and become awkward and unsure of themselves. More than 90 percent of women in America have a negative body image and find themselves to be lacking in some area.

My "body image" is not what I see in the mirror. It is what I see in my head; it is my mind's picture of how I look. An amazing phenomenon has been discovered in many weight-loss clinics. When a client loses pounds and pounds of weight, she often still sees herself in her mind as a fat person, and consequently responds to the world from this point of view.

I have a friend who experienced this kind of distorted body image—not with her weight, but with the size of her nose. Jean had a perfectly good nose, as far as I could see, but to her it was huge. Like the man in the sinus spray commercial, when Jean looked in the mirror she saw nothing but a big nose walking around. So she had reconstructive surgery—a "nose job." But she recently confessed to me that she now is surprised every time she looks in the mirror and sees her tiny, perfect nose. Her body image still has that old, big one.

With the exception of my pregnancies, I cannot remember a time in my life when I have felt confident about my body. Even as far back as the age of twelve and thirteen, I dreaded the coming of summer, the season of shorts and swimsuits. I was too fat, my stomach pooched out, my hips were too wide; my friends looked great, I looked awful.

As I write this, I get out some of my old picture albums and look through snapshots of me and Nancy Lewis at her family's lake cabin. There we are, smiling on the dock, with our beach towels and our bottles of Sun-In. And I am surprised to see not one skinny, knobby-kneed girl in a bikini, but two. Where did I ever get the idea that I was fat?

I'll tell you where I got it. I got it by doing what every other American teenage girl was doing in the summer of '69. I was poring over pictures of Cheryl Tiegs and all those other models smiling out at me from the pages of *Seventeen* magazine, and I was comparing myself. I was letting the media whisper its fantasies to me, and the reality I saw in the mirror couldn't compare. I was thirteen; my body hadn't even developed yet; and I'd already decided it wasn't good enough. I was playing that dead-end game, "If Only."

And in my weak moments I find myself, twenty-three years later, still playing that game; I've just graduated to *Vogue* and *McCall's*.

Why do I have such a hard time loving my body? I love my husband's body. I love the shape of it, the smell of it, the familiarity of it. I love my children's wiggly bodies. I love Seth's long, lanky legs and Matt's stout, sturdy little torso. I love the feel of their skin; I marvel at their perfect beauty. Why can't I marvel at myself? Why can't you?

Because our standard is skewed. The magazines have lied to us. We are like victims of pornography. We have looked at the glossy pictures so long that looking in the mirror is painful.

CREATED IN HIS IMAGE

Our bodies were created for a far more glorious purpose than just to look good. If that's the sole criteria by which we judge our worth, then we've cheated ourselves. We've bound ourselves to one tiny portion of our potential. We are made for so much more!

I have felt the freedom of this discovery with each of my pregnancies. Suddenly, I was free of all those fashion rules—no belts, no waistlines, no tummy-flattening Lycra. My body was a miracle. My breasts were no longer just ornamental; they had a function! My blood was pumping. I was eating healthy, not to be thin, but to give life to another little being. To me, my stomach was a status symbol, a badge of honor.

Why? Because for the first time I was seeing my body through something other than the critical eye of fashion. I saw my body through the eyes of my Creator, who lovingly made me and who thinks I am beautiful. And not because of how I look, but because of what I am: formed in his image, a reflection of him.

God himself fashioned our bodies. Let me take you aside here to tell you that for seven long years I went through the painful struggle of infertility after I lost a Fallopian tube to Toxic Shock Syndrome in college. My children are quite literally miracles. Perhaps that's why pregnancy was so amazing and joyful for me—and why I can't ever take motherhood for granted. I will never forget those years of disappointment and self-accusation as month after month my body failed to function in what I perceived as its most fundamentally feminine aspect: bearing children. What kind of woman was I?

See, there is another cruel standard by which we judge our bodies besides that of form—and that is function. Too often, those of us who can't have children or nurse them successfully or enjoy lovemaking or live with our hormones feel betrayed by our bodies, like failed experiments, poor specimens, or damaged goods. We feel like something went wrong when we were being designed. And that also is a lie.

God himself fashioned our bodies. I love James Weldon Johnson's description of God, "like a Mammy bending over her baby," toiling with a piece of clay to make us just right. This creation was more intricate, more special than all the others, because this one was a tiny model of the

Creator himself. He gave us hands so that we could be craftsmen, building and making just like the One who made us. He added strong legs and arms so that we could lift, carry, build, climb, run, hunt, jump. He gave us intricate brains so that we could think and communicate, respond to our world; emotions so that we could feel and develop relationships and love, just as he does. He gave us bodies that could nurture and protect, defend and rule, touch and feel, change and age, and in all these things help us to understand and love our Creator as we come to understand and love ourselves.

There is so much to love about ourselves. But too often, like the children of Israel who made themselves a golden calf to worship, we have made our own idol—a golden image of the Ideal Woman—and dedicated ourselves to the impossible and unrewarding task of reflecting its image instead of God's.

MAKING PEACE WITH OUR BODIES

Our struggle to make peace with the realities of our bodies begins when we surrender those pornographic, distorted standards we have set for ourselves. To God we give all the painful images of not being good enough, thin enough, tall enough, pretty enough, sexy enough. And we ask for his healing. Give us new eyes, we pray, with which to see ourselves. Help us see our bodies, our hands, our feet, our faces, through the eyes of the One who made them.

We surrender our struggle to get through life without its leaving a mark on us—to always look as new and fresh as we did at the beginning. Like the Velveteen Rabbit, who dreaded the thought of becoming loose in the joints and shabby, we wish we could become real without all those uncomfortable things happening to us. But life just doesn't work that way. If we want to have a real, honest, fulfilling existence, we must surrender ourselves to the effects of life, to the passing of time. These are inevitable, and our struggle to resist is silly. Give us grace, we pray, not eternal youth. Help us to see, like the commercial says, that we are not older, but better. Help us to embrace what we are becoming, to welcome each age for the "new things" it will bring us.

Only then can we make peace with our bodies . . . with the nose we inherited from our father's side; with the hips that all the women in our family have; with stretch marks that are reminders of the miracle of childbirth or wrinkles that weren't there two years ago; with limbs that move more slowly and joints that creak more; with a body that is individually, irreplaceably, for better or worse, uniquely ours.

FINDING A REASON TO CELEBRATE

As Matt's nursery song goes, "I'm the only me God made; there's nobody quite like me." There is joy in this thought! There is wonder, there is something to celebrate.

Nobody else has my laugh. No one has my walk, my sense of humor, my particular way of doing things. No one else has all those years of making love with my husband, the way we fit together, moving almost from memory, knowing the little things. No one else has rocked these babies, watched their bodies grow and change, nursed them and tended them. The lines, the wrinkles—those represent a life of experience and memory, a life lived only by me, only as I could live it, only with this body that is God's gift to me. What better reason to celebrate?

Celebrate as Christ did, by being broken. God sent himself in human form to make himself real to us. He was a man, with a body. But the Scriptures never tell us what Jesus looked like. What is important is what Jesus did with his body. He used it. He spent it. And finally, he sacrificed it.

Christ is our example. There is no joy, no celebration, no freedom in preserving ourselves, keeping ourselves carefully back, ornamental and cold upon our shelves. There is joy in being used, in being vessels, in being broken to spill out the fragrance of Christ on everyone we touch. There is freedom in dying . . . in dying to adolescence and becoming young women, in dying through childbirth and giving new life, in dying to our youth and finding the joy of a new age, in dying to our vanity and discovering a new kind of beauty.

A BEAUTIFUL WOMAN

I have given you a picture of my mother as someone with Horrible Hair, but let me now tell you that my mother's hair really is lovely. She wears it up in a knot, like Katharine Hepburn. Some strands are always escaping.

My mother is an elegant woman, whether she is dressed in silk or in a T-shirt. She does not have beautiful fingernails; she does have beautiful blue eyes, and a face that has aged with incredible grace and loveliness. I have never seen her try to be something she is not; at every stage of her life, she has simply been who she is. She is a lady of great poise who is quite willing to squat down in the grass to admire a ladybug with her grandson.

I have pictures of my mother at our family's river cabin, in her sun hat and old swimsuit, standing with her feet in the cold current. She is not the thinnest person in the picture, nor the youngest. Others have better figures and deeper tans. To me, however, she is the most beautiful.

She gazes out at me, a graceful reflection of God's glory. Her sense of self inspires me. I look at her, and I remember other pictures I have of her in my memory: young and slim, as fashionable as Jackie Kennedy in her Easter suit; tramping through the woods on a Camp Fire Girl retreat; laughing and tan on the beach in Florida. I remember how glamorous she seemed, all dressed up for a Saturday night out with Dad; how wonderful she smelled; how comforting it was to have her come crawl into bed with me when I was scared in the middle of the night. I remember how I admired her, how I played dress-up with her makeup and jewelry and her old formals, yearning to grow up and be just like her.

And I do have my mother's eyes, her hair, some of her style. We kind of smile alike. There is a lot of me that is her.

As I write this, I am expecting the birth of my third child in about a week. I remember how I felt when I first laid eyes on the other two. I knew they were mine because of their little mouths; there was nobody else they could have gotten those mouths from. Their strange little faces somehow looked familiar. "Wow! I thought, that's a part of me." How amazing.

And you and I must realize that our bodies also bear a family resemblance—to a heavenly Father who created us in his image. A Father who labored over each one of us to make us each uniquely like him in some way. A Father who, when we were born, stepped back and said to himself, "Wow! Will you look at that. That's a part of me."

How amazing!

For Thou didst form my inward parts;
Thou didst weave me in my mother's womb.
I will give thanks to Thee,
for I am fearfully and wonderfully made;
Wonderful are Thy works,
And my soul knows it very well.
My frame was not hidden from Thee,
When I was made in secret,
And skillfully wrought in the depths of the earth.
Thine eyes have seen my unformed substance;
And in Thy book they were all written,
The days that were ordained for me,
When as yet there was not one of them.

PSALM 139:13–16 NASB

Celebrate Yourself

Get out your family albums and spend a few moments
looking back at your heritage. Whose nose did you inherit?
Whose smile? Whose eyes? Whose sense of humor?

Look back at how you have changed over the years: holidays,
weddings, graduations, birthdays, babies, vacations,
the fat periods, the skinny periods, the bad hairdos.
You, and only you, have lived these moments.
Thank God for who he has made you to be.

*Father Creator, forgive me for failing to marvel
at your handiwork in me. Thank you for making
this amazing body! Teach me how to love it
as you love it. Help me to learn to care for it
and cherish it, not to make it an idol.
Show me how my body is a reflection of you,
and free me to celebrate that reflection.*

AMEN

FOUR

A Kiss for the Frog Prince

Claire's chapter about good days, rotten days, and amazing grace

Every day I watch the way you struggle,
rushing through the rituals and pushing through the days.
Listen to the still, small voice that calls you,
come away into my arms of faithfulness and grace.

I love you for free—
no strings attached and no holds barred.
I love you for free—
I paid everything I am to purchase everything you are.
Let my spirit give you eyes to see—
I love you for free.

You don't have to try to earn my mercy.
Don't you know that I've already bled to pay the price?
You're the one I loved enough to die for;
you're the reason I was such a willing sacrifice.

I love you for free—
no strings attached and no holds barred.
I love you for free—
I paid everything I am to purchase everything you are.
Let my spirit give you eyes to see—
I love you for free.

No one took my life from me, I freely poured it out.
I was paying for the chance to say the words I'm saying now—

I love you for free—
no strings attached and no holds barred.
I love you for free—
I paid everything I am to purchase everything you are.
Let my spirit give you eyes to see—
I love you for free.

CLAIRE CLONINGER AND JAMIE HARVILL[1]

In my life there are good days and there are bad days. On a good day, I can really feel God's love. It's almost tangible.

On a good day, I wake up early. I run three or four miles. I have a long and meaningful prayer time. I am out in the office writing by nine o'clock, and I have wonderful ideas which I translate into a song or a chapter certain to change somebody's life for the better. I eat leafy green and yellow vegetables, and when offered gooey deserts I smile and say "no thank you." I do not watch TV. I feel charitable toward the members of my family and say encouraging things all day long. I am kind to friends, strangers, and small animals. In the evening, I cook a meal in which nothing burns or is underdone. I wash the dishes and plump the pillows on the sofa and take a warm bath and put on a clean nightie and fall self-righteously into bed, thinking, "Of course God loves me. What's not to love? I am a doll!"

But a bad day is a very different story. On a bad day, I wake up late and growl before my eyes are fully open. I figure I've already missed my prayer time, so I scratch it. I am cross with my husband, my sons, my neighbors, my friends, salespersons in stores, people in traffic, and innocent children. I gossip about people I should be praying for. I make resolutions to stop doing that, and the next time the phone rings, I'm at it again. I watch hours of TV and eat mounds of potato chips. I do not write a word nor move a muscle, and by the time I turn out the light at night, there is only one word to describe me: *yuk*. Not only do I not love myself, but I find it impossible to believe that God, Jesus, or anyone even remotely associated with heaven could locate a kind thought to send my way. I mean, some days it gets severe.

The story of my good days and my bad days demonstrates something unfortunate and skewed about my expectations of God. I keep expecting him to act like me. I keep expecting him to love like I love. I keep expecting him to give me what I think I deserve. And, of course, he doesn't.

ONLY ONE SPEED

But what is the truth about my good day and my bad day where God is concerned? On which day would you figure he loves me the most, on a scale of one to ten? Actually, as you might have guessed, it's the same—exactly the same. On a scale of one to ten, God loves me a ten on my best day and a ten on my worst day.

How can he do that? How can he get away with being so indiscriminate? I think it has something to do with the fact that he's God, and his capacity to love is not dependent in any way on my ability to perform.

Better go over that one again. It's a biggie. God's love is not dependent on my performance. It is not rationed out to me in proportion to my goodness or my badness on any given day.

His capacity to love is linked instead to the fact that his whole nature is totally turned toward love. In fact, *he is love*. He's made out of it. He's overflowing with it. Love is his composition and his contents. Love is his definition and his job description. It's his occupation and his preoccupation. It's his mission and his passion and his favorite pastime. Love is who God is and what he does.

And God's love comes in only one speed: ten. *Ten*. Crank it up. Floorboard it. Pedal to the metal. Full speed ahead. Good days, bad days, and in-between days, it's coming at me. Paid for and free for the asking, full to overflowing, broken and poured out. I didn't earn it, I don't deserve it, there's no way I can ever pay it back, and yet it's mine.

What's more, there's no way I can lose God's love by what I do or don't do. And there is no way I can improve it by what I do or don't do. There's nothing I can do to make him love me less and nothing I can do to make him love me more.

Amazing, you say? You bet it is! It is, quite simply, the best-kept secret of the Christian life, the much-discussed but little-understood mystery we call "amazing grace."

WHAT WE DESERVE AND WHAT WE GET

I've spent a large part of my Christian journey trying to get a handle on grace. As a child of this performance-oriented culture, which gives its rewards to the high achievers and the first-place finishers, I must admit I stand open-mouthed at the very idea of a God who loves me "just because." I feel amazed and tongue-tied and more than a tad uncomfortable to find myself presented with a prize I didn't win, a reward I didn't earn, and an astounding reality I must sometimes struggle to internalize.

What do I deserve if not grace? Theologically speaking, I deserve hell—since by God's standard of measurement anything short of perfection gets a thumbs down.

Comedian and singer Mark Lowry realized this when he was griping to God about not getting paid what he deserved after a performance. After his griping had died down for a minute, Mark sensed God saying, "Mark, if you got what you deserved, it would be pure hell."

Based on that experience, Tommy Greer and I wrote a tongue-in-cheek song for Mark to use in concert. In the lingo of the comedian, it expresses Mark's theological revelation about not getting what we deserve:

> When the market's plunging and inflation peaks,
> When your in-laws drop in to spend the week,
> When the rain keeps pouring through the roof that leaks
> And you don't feel very well;
> When your job is throwing you a major curve,
> And all your friends begin to work your nerves,
> It's mild compared to what you deserve,
> 'Cause what you deserve is hell!
>
> And it sure beats hell, it sure beats hell!
> Considering where you could be now, you're doing pretty well.
> So count your blessings, dude; work up some gratitude;
> You know, you could be barbecued,
> And it sure beats hell, it sure beats hell.
> You could be checking in tonight to Lucifer's motel.
> So don't be a thankless slob; Jesus Christ has done the job
> And you're not a shish-kabob,
> And that sure beats hell![2]

PLAYING BY THE WRONG RULE BOOK

So don't get me wrong. Even though the idea of grace sometimes makes me feel uncomfortable, considering the alternatives, I'm delighted to receive it!

It's just that sometimes I feel like I've spent most of my life trying to measure up, to earn and achieve and be good enough. And then, suddenly, I am confronted with this incredible Person who loves me anyway—no matter what. And it's a little like being somewhere near the middle of the third quarter and abruptly realizing I've been playing by the wrong rule book all the time! All the yardage I thought I had gained early in the game (by striving to achieve) has not done a thing to improve my position. God would have loved me anyway!

I don't think I'm alone in my failure to grasp God's overriding law of grace. Let's face it; our culture does little to prepare us for the idea of it. Even those of us from the most nurturing childhoods have had to learn how to operate under the terms of "conditional love." Parents, teachers, and society in general have made us understand that the world likes a good little girl. If we want to be liked, therefore, it would be wise to be as good as possible.

Even the most loving parents attach conditions to their approval and their rewards, at least some of the time: "You can do this *if* you do that," and so forth. I'm not blaming anybody here; I'm just saying how it is.

And for that reason, because we have not had a whole lot of experience with the totally unconditional nature of grace, we often find it baffling.

A PICTURE OF GRACE

Victor Hugo's great novel, *Les Misérables*, includes an unforgettable scene in which a man finds himself totally bewildered by an unexpected touch of grace. Jean Valjean, the main character of the story, has been released from prison after serving years for merely stealing a loaf of bread. He spends his first night of freedom in the home of kindly old Bishop Myriel. There he is given the first good meal, the first clean clothes, and the first comfortable bed he has known in years. Valjean, distrustful of the bishop's kindness, thanks his benefactor by stealing his silver dishes.

When Valjean is captured by the police and returned to the home of the Bishop, he naturally expects to be charged with theft. To his surprise, however, the compassionate Myriel tells the policeman that the silver plates had not been stolen at all, but presented as a gift to Valjean. The kind old clergyman refuses to press charges.

Then to heap grace upon grace, Bishop Myriel lifts the heavy silver candlesticks off the mantel and hands them to Valjean, saying, in effect, "Here, Jean, you forgot to take these candlesticks, which I also meant for you to have."

This is a picture of grace. It is kindness we did not expect and generosity we did not deserve. It is a gift we could never earn from a friend of whom we are not worthy. And when it comes unexpectedly into our lives, if we've been playing the game out of another rule book, it can be difficult to understand, and awkward to accept. We stand dumbstruck, fumbling for the proper response.

A SPIRITUAL DUNCE CAP

It would seem that, after all the grace I've received in my lifetime, I would know the proper response by now. But grace is a lesson I keep having to learn over and over again.

When I decided to turn my life over to the Lord on a January night fifteen years ago, I understood grace perfectly—and I knew it was exactly what I needed. To begin with, I knew I was out of answers of my own. I knew I was about as needy as I had ever been. It was easy to see myself as a drowning refugee cast in turbulent waters because, spiritually, that's exactly what I was. I was splashing and sputtering and dog-paddling as hard as I could, and still I was slipping under the waves. It was easy for me to know that I needed a savior, and I grabbed at the grace God held out to me like a life preserver. But once the Lord had gotten me to shore, gotten the water out of my lungs, and dried me off, I thanked him profusely and said, in effect, "I'm okay now. I'll take it from here. You've done the hard part, now I'll take over. I'm going to live for you now and be a really good person. Not to worry. Leave it to me."

Then, without even realizing it, I went right back to struggling in my own strength—with only one slight alteration. I went from my old routine of dancing for the approval of the world to dancing for the approval of God and his people. I went from my old litany of "shoulds" and "oughts" to a new and sanctified set.

Like the little pig leaving home to make his fortune in the world, I set out to make good in this new kingdom. Since performance had always earned points for me in the old kingdom, I saw no reason to abandon that game plan. So I set out, on some unconscious level, to "perform" spiritually. (Look, I know this sounds silly. It *is* silly. But that's how clueless I was.)

Most mornings, as I entered my prayer time with the Lord, I felt the pressure of some intangible quota I had to meet. I felt obliged to chalk up a certain number of minutes per day or hours per week, though no one was keeping score but me.

Then there was the "quality gauge" I unconsciously attached to my spiritual experiences. On days when I felt that I had really heard from God, really stated my case well to him, really enjoyed the praise and gotten a lot out of the Bible reading, I felt fantastic. But at other times, when nothing much seemed to have happened, I felt like a failure.

And then there were the mornings when, exhausted from the ongoing demands of children and career, I would get up early for a quiet time with the Lord and actually fall asleep with my face in the Bible. I'd wake up to find that I had been drooling into the pages of 2 Chronicles. At times like that, I felt certain that Billy Graham, Mother Teresa, and other spiritual giants were sitting on the front row as God's favorites, and I was in the corner wearing a dunce cap.

A HUNDRED-POUND BACKPACK

When I look back at my workaholic determination to earn God's approval and my inability to understand his grace, I am reminded of the old story of the traveler with the hundred-pound backpack:

> A road-weary traveler had walked all day carrying a hundred-pound pack on his back. Finally, after many miles, a sturdy, horse-drawn wagon pulled up alongside, and the driver offered the poor traveler a ride. Gratefully accepting the offer, the traveler climbed wearily into the cart beside the driver, but he refused to take the heavy bundle off of his back.
>
> "Please, sir," the driver encouraged his passenger, "Won't you put your heavy bundle down? There is ample room in my cart for it, and I know that your shoulders must be aching from the load."
>
> "Never mind," the traveler replied. "I can carry it. I'm very used to it, you see." And so on he rode, still stupidly shouldering the back-breaking load.[3]

Little by little, I am learning to put down the back-breaking load of self-effort and enjoy the ride. Gently, patiently, again and again, God keeps taking me back to the drawing board on the subject of grace. With enormous perseverance and a good sense of humor, he continues my higher education in the classroom of his mercy. And though I am thick-headed and more than a little bit stubborn, I have gradually realized many things.

THE ROCK IN MY PINAFORE POCKET

One thing I've realized is that I had experienced hundreds of touches of grace before I ever tried to understand the term. And one of the first grace-filled moments I can remember happened when I was only six.

My first-grade teacher was a lovely, white-haired, grandmotherly woman named Mrs. Sullivan whose classroom was full of wonderful things. But the best of all was a dazzling rock collection that she kept attractively displayed on the shelves behind her desk.

All of us kids loved that rock collection. Some days, if we finished our desk work ahead of time, we were permitted to walk up and down in front of the shelves, admire the rocks with their different shapes and colors, and try to read the identifying cards with their mysterious names. But we knew the rules. We could look, but we had better not touch!

My favorite rock of all was the most impressive one in the collection. It sparkled with what seemed to be a million different planes and facets. It was crystal clear with a slightly pinkish cast. It was beautiful.

One winter afternoon, when I had finished my desk work early and was standing alone behind Mrs. Sullivan's desk, admiring my favorite rock, I was suddenly overwhelmed by a desire to pick it up. The next thing I knew, I had put it in the pocket of my pinafore!

My heart pounded like a sledgehammer. I felt like my whole body had a violent case of hiccups! My cheeks burned, and I was terrified at my predicament. I knew I couldn't keep the rock, but I didn't know how to put it back without being noticed.

I walked home that afternoon as I usually did, but I was so upset that by the time I reached my front door, I threw it open and ran sobbing into my mother's arms.

"I've taken a rock from Mrs. Sullivan's rock collection," I blurted out tearfully, "and you've gotta go and put it back, Mom."

My mother had a great opportunity for a lecture at that point, but I think she could see I didn't need to be convinced of my guilt. Instead of scolding, she held me and comforted me and thanked me for my honest confession. Then, in a very gentle voice, she told me that I would have to return the rock myself and apologize to Mrs. Sullivan.

I died a million deaths. I anguished. I pleaded with her to do it for me. But she was already getting the car keys and leading me to the car. Before I knew it, we were on our way back to school. Mom parked the car and walked me as far as the classroom door.

A LITTLE CHIP OF GRACE

I can see that classroom as clearly in my mind's eye today as I saw it that afternoon. The desks were empty, but the overhead lights were still on, and Mrs. Sullivan was at her desk. Slowly I approached the desk, holding the pink crystal rock like a burning coal in my hand.

"Mrs. Sullivan," I almost whispered, and she looked up at me. "I took your rock," I said, holding it out to her and feeling my eyes begin to burn again. "I'm sorry," I said . . . and began to sob.

I remember how surprised I was to realize that Mrs. Sullivan had put her arms around me and was comforting me just as my mother had. Her reaction wasn't at all what I had expected.

"I'm very proud of you, Claire," she said softly. "Returning the rock was the right thing to do, and you did it right away. I'm very proud of you."

What she did next was the tenderest, kindest thing I could ever have imagined. Over all of these years, it melts my heart to remember it. She took me by the hand and told my mother that we would be right back. Then we walked together down the hall to the little supply room, where we found our school janitor, Mr. Pete.

"Mr. Pete," she said to him, handing him the pink crystal rock. I want Claire to have a little piece of this rock to keep. Do you think you could chip one off for her?"

"I sure could," he said, and that's exactly what he did.

In some way that I didn't fully understand at the time, that rock became very important to me. It was more than a pretty rock, more than a favorite possession. Holding it was like having, in my hands, a little chip of grace.

Those who dispense grace to others often do more than they know they are doing. I received so much that day. I received a blessing and a lesson from my mother, whose grace that day was not cheap. She forgave me and loved me, but she didn't spare me the pain of owning up to my crime. She loved me enough to make me stand up and do the right thing.

And I received a different kind of blessing from Mrs. Sullivan. She forgave me, too, and affirmed me, but she did more than that. Her grace went beyond forgiveness to mercy. She let me know that I was very important to her. More important, in fact, than the rules I had broken, and more important than her treasured possession, which I had pocketed and gone home with. By her willingness to chip off a part of that pink crystal treasure for me, my teacher was saying, "You mean more to me than anything I own."

GLIMPSES OF GRACE

Jesus always saw the importance and affirmed the value of the individual.

When others saw a woman caught in adultery, a sinner ripe for stoning, he saw a desperate and wounded soul in need of forgiveness, a potential saint who was capable of higher things.[4]

When his disciples would have sent the noisy, dusty crowd of little children away, Jesus stopped everything he was doing. He smiled and opened his arms and said, "Come unto me." And as he picked them up and set them on his knee, everything about him was saying, "You matter to me. You're not a nuisance. You are a treasure."[5]

When the parade of life was passing by the little man who had climbed up in the tree, Jesus stopped the parade and called up, "Come down, Zacchaeus. You matter to me. It's you I want to have supper with tonight."[6]

When the one they had always shunned and called "maniac" and "demon child" fell foaming and raving at his feet, Jesus saw something that the others could not see. He saw the desperate prisoner inside the mad disguise, the man in need of mercy. And he called that man forth to be calm and clothed and in his right mind.[7]

Jesus was a constant dispenser of grace. He extended his hand to demoniacs and lepers and prostitutes and beggars. He ate with tax collectors and sinners. He said with his life, "There are no unimportant people. Every one is valuable to my Father and to me."

And his final and definitive word on the value of our lives was spoken wordlessly as he allowed his tortured body to be nailed to a cross for us—for our selfishness and our sinfulness and our pigheaded determination to live life by our own rules.

THE LANGUAGE OF GRACE

Grace always speaks the language of Calvary. It always affirms the value of the individual. Grace says, "You are important." More important than your standing or your position. More important than your wrong choices or your destructive behavior.

Grace says, "I see beyond the outward appearance and into your heart, and I believe you are worth whatever I have to go through to make things right on your behalf."

Grace says, "Come in. It's safe to take your mask off here. It's you we want—not the shiny, competent façade you've erected. Not your defense mechanisms or your clever conversation or your efforts to impress. It's you we care about—the real you."

Grace speaks a gospel of hope to the hopeless and help to the helpless, a gospel of joy to the brokenhearted and comfort to the wounded, a gospel of freedom to the prisoner and new beginnings to the one whose heart has hit a dead end.

This is the gospel that Brennen Manning has dubbed "the ragamuffin gospel"—a gospel not for the Pharisee or the spiritually muscle-bound, not for the "fearless and the tearless," but a gospel which stoops to embrace

> the bedraggled, beat-up, and burnt-out . . . the wobbly and weak-kneed who know they don't have it altogether . . . the poor, weak, sinful men and women with hereditary faults and limited talents . . . the earthen vessels who shuffle along on feet of clay . . . the smart people who know they are stupid and the honest disciples who know they are scalawags.[8]

This is a gospel that reaches down into the heart of your life and of mine. This is very good news indeed!

KISSING THE FROG

Would it surprise you to know that the "ragamuffin gospel" is the theme of one of my favorite fairy tales? There are no glass slippers in this quaint little parable of grace. It's the story of a toad of a guy who longs for somebody to love him, warts and all. It is called "The Frog Prince."

In "The Frog Prince," a beautiful princess develops an unlikely friendship with a talkative frog who lives in her pond. She grows so fond of him, in fact, that one day she bends down and plants a big kiss on his green and warty lips. Magically, that kiss breaks a wicked spell, and the frog turns into a handsome and lovable prince. Of course, you know where the story goes from there. "Happily ever after" is a foregone conclusion.

God's grace comes to us a lot like that kiss. It comes to us exactly as we are, warts and all. And when it does, it totally rewrites our rule books. It tells us we are loved and prized and very, very worth it, just as we are.

It also tells us that on our best days and on our worst days we are valuable to God, regardless of whether we *feel* valuable. It teaches us to trust God's opinion of us rather than our own feelings about ourselves. And that's important, because I have come to the conclusion that, in this country, feelings are highly overrated.

Remember that cabaret song entitled "Feelings," which obtained enormous popularity in this country some years ago for reasons that have always eluded me? You know, the one that goes, "feelings, woooooooh, feelings"?

Well, if I had written this song, I would be a lot richer than I am today. But I'm glad I didn't, because I don't believe that feelings deserve to have their own theme song. It seems to me that there are already too many people in this country worshiping at the shrine of feelings.

Yes, I know that feelings are a gift from God. And I'm thankful for mine; I'm glad I can feel things. I wouldn't want to live a life without feelings.

But feelings were never meant to direct the course of our lives. Feelings are a faulty compass that lead us around and around in circles and finally back to ourselves. They lead us to be self-absorbed navel gazers unable to navigate outside of our own perspective.

God's grace, on the other hand, is the compass we can trust. Like the North Star, it is always true. It keeps us looking up into the amazing and unshakable stellar truths of who we are in heaven's sight: we're his kids, his creations, his children, his own. And he is certifiably nuts about us!

God's grace frees us from the prison of seeking inner contentment by trying to be good enough. And it releases us into the wonder and joy that Abraham Heschel must have felt when he wrote the words, "Just to be is a blessing. Just to live is holy."[9]

God's grace invites us into an intimate love relationship with the One who died so that we could live. It says, "I no longer call you servants, because a servant does not know his master's business. Instead, I have called you friends."[10] It opens the door to prayer that is conversation and praise that is as natural as breathing.

And, like the kiss of the princess that transformed the frog, grace transforms us. It transforms our lives of struggling and striving and approval seeking into lives of sanity and serenity and something worth celebrating.

Even when the glass slipper doesn't fit and the silver spoon is in somebody else's mouth.

For it is by grace you have been saved,
through faith—and this not from yourselves,
it is the gift of God—
not by works, so that no one can boast.
For we are God's workmanship, created in
Christ Jesus to do good works,
which God prepared in advance for us to do.

EPHESIANS 2:8–10 NIV

For it is God who is at work within you,
giving you the will and the power
to achieve his purpose.

PHILIPPIANS 2:13 PHILLIPS

Celebrate God's Grace

Look back at your life and remember some of your own
"rock in the pinafore pocket" experiences—
times you received something good you did not deserve.
How have these incidents of grace shaped you and
made you who you are?

Look at this day as a gift of grace and take time
to appreciate the little grace-filled moments
and activities you tend to take for granted.
Enjoy the sunshine, a cup of coffee, a visit with a friend.
Thank God all day long for his many "tender mercies."
And enjoy the blessing that goes with
extending mercy to someone else.

During your prayer time, write God a letter
and thank him for his grace in your life,
beginning with the gracious gift of his Son.

*O Father, I thank you for giving me not what my sin merits,
but what your love decrees; not what I expect or deserve,
but what you know I need.
Help me to put down the heavy load of self-effort
and receive the reality of your unconditional love,
which re-creates me in your image.
Help me to see your hand of grace all around me,
in the circumstances and people you bring into my life.
May your grace in me be contagious, Lord.
May it spread from my life to others around me.*

AMEN

FIVE

Bibbidy-Bobbidy-Boo

Karla's chapter about
doing it all—and what to do
when it does you in

❧

Whirlwind days, with life on the run:
put out a fire, while another starts burning.
Catch your breath; the work's never done.
When will the wheels ever stop all their turning?

Tell him your sorrow,
lean on his care.
Fall on his promise to be there.

Do you love him?
Tell him so.
Do you need him?
Tell him so.
Do you love him?
Then just tell him so.
Are you weary?
Tell him so.
Is your heart heavy?
Tell him so.
Jesus hears you.
Tell him so.

KARLA WORLEY AND TIM SHEPPARD[1]

O ne lazy summer afternoon, my neighbor and I were sitting out in the backyard, watching our toddlers splash in their little, green-plastic wading pool and generally reflecting on the meaning of life—or, rather, our lives. It was Linda's tenth wedding anniversary, and we had decided it would be fun to get out her wedding pictures and look through them.

"You know," she sighed, "when they send you out the door of the church, they shouldn't dress you in a long, white dress and veil. They should give you a big, red cape and a suit with an *S* on the chest, 'cause that's what you're going to need!"

Where did we get the idea that we have to be Superwoman—able to do it all with grace and efficiency?

Was it from June Cleaver, in her pearls and heels, baking cookies for Ward and the Beaver? Or Scarlett O'Hara, ("As God is my witness, I'll never be hungry again!") saving her family by the clever use of her living room drapes? Or how about Nancy Drew, teen Superwoman, who could sleuth around in dusty attics and still dress in time for the dinner dance? Or Jane Fonda, who taught us we could be politically active and look great in leg warmers? Or, worst of all, that awful woman in the TV ad who can "bring home the bacon, fry it up in a pan, and never, never let him forget he's a man"?

Take your pick. Superwoman role models abound.

MY FIRST ROLE MODEL

I myself got the impression that "real women can do it all" from my mother. Because, quite frankly, she can.

She cooks (from scratch). She sews (without a pattern). She gardens (from seeds). She decorates (without a consultant). She plays tennis (on the first-string team). She has a professional career, does her own hair, reads a lot, volunteers, throws parties, goes out to dinner, charms my dad after all these years, and even hangs her laundry out to dry because "it smells better than when you put it in a dryer."

And, of course, she doesn't look her age. For her birthday, Dad gave her a T-shirt that reads, "Still Perfect after All These Years."

It isn't easy to have a mom like that. I tried to tell her this once, in one of those "mother-daughter" moments you have. (Ours usually happen in the kitchen, while putting away dishes.)

"It's pretty intimidating to have a mom like you," I tried to explain. "I mean, you do everything perfectly."

"Nonsense. I am not perfect," she snapped. "I'm perfectly normal."

See, she even does normal perfectly.

It's enough to give me a complex—especially when I try to live up to her standards.

NOT-SO-GREAT EXPECTATIONS

For the first three years Dennis and I were married, I gave it my best effort. I cooked (Mom's recipes). I sewed (with patterns . . . Simplicity!). I antiqued and refinished; I made drapes; I planted flowers. I did not take up tennis, but I did rent Jane Fonda videos and aerobicized instead. I had a full-time job, cleaned the bathrooms, washed Dennis's socks, and did my own hair. Finally one night, I sat in the middle of the bathroom floor and screamed at my innocent husband.

"I cannot do it all!" I sobbed. "It's unreasonable for you to expect it of me."

"I don't expect it of you," Dennis said. "*You* expect it of you. You are not your mother, and until you come to grips with that fact, you are going to keep driving yourself crazy."

Well, I must admit . . . for a guy who most of the time can't even make his own ham sandwich, Dennis sure has his moments; and when he does, they are pretty piercing. He was right; I'm not my Mother. And over the years, I've gradually gotten it through my head that that's okay. I hate to sew, but I love to garden. I'm a great cook, but I'm pretty lousy at cleaning up. I hate tennis. I like the way clothes smell out of the dryer. And I can't do my own hair, but I have a friend at a nearby styling salon who does. Accepting all the differences has helped me to love myself, and it has also helped me to love my mother for the great woman she is.

BECOMING AN OVERACHIEVER

Chances are that you, too, are reacting to your mother's way of doing things. My mother is reacting to her mother. Most of us are trying desperately either to be exactly like our mothers—or nothing at all like them. My best friend's mom was an alcoholic, an emotional incompetent. Cindy has spent her adult life proving that she is just the opposite.

Our mothers, in one way or another, made us who we are. So did our fathers. The way our parents raised us, taught us, loved us (or didn't) has a profound impact on our self-image and our achievements. So does a lot of other things—our inborn temperament, the region where we grow up. Even our birth order is a factor.

I was a first child. A "good" child. The one who sought to please. The one who took the first steps, made the first grades, went on the first dates, left home first. Maybe it was hard to be my little brother and follow along. But believe me, it wasn't easy to be first, either.

Report cards were a big deal at my house. My parents expected *A*s. When I made a *B*, they sat me down and asked me just what had happened here. Why hadn't I done my best?

I remember once telling my dad that Nancy Lewis got a dollar for every *A* she got on her report card, and what did he think of that idea?

"I'll tell you what," he replied. "Why don't you try making something other than an *A* and see what you get?"

You can see how they looked at things.

In our house, the worst thing you could be was average. And that kind of a standard has both a good and a bad side. Working "above average" is a great goal. But it can also be daunting; it can make you afraid to try at all. I dropped out of a couple of classes in college because it was obvious I wasn't going to make a good grade. It seemed better to get out than just to just get by. Now, looking back, I wonder how much I missed by not attempting what I couldn't excel in.

I see this attitude in my oldest son, Seth. Like me, he's a firstborn, and a perfectionist. He has the hardest time practicing his piano lessons, because he hates to make a mistake. Sometimes he hesitates to try a new song because he can't get it right the first time.

But Dennis and I are trying hard to downplay accomplishment in our house and to emphasize effort. To teach our children that sometimes things are worth doing for their own sake—not just to be the best. (To me, there is a distinct difference between being the best and doing your best. We can't let anything else set the standards for our success—in career, in marriage, in parenting, in weight loss, or anything else. We can't compare our success to our neighbor's, or to our relative's, or to some example held up to us in the latest "how to" course. Everybody's best effort is different.)

And the thing is, in real life, you can't always drop the course in midsemester if things aren't going well. There are some things you have to keep doing, even if you find you're not going to make an *A*—like laundry, or housekeeping, or cooking. Like parenting or marriage.

Superwoman, in other words, is a myth, and it's time we all got this through our heads. We are all good at some things and not so good at others. Nobody can do it all—especially not perfectly, and certainly not all at once!

A TIME FOR EVERYTHING

I used to hate that "excellent wife" described in Proverbs 31:10. She "works with her hands. . . . brings her food from afar. . . . rises also while it is still night. . . . considers a field and buys it. . . . extends her hand to the poor. . . . Her clothing is fine linen. . . . She smiles at the future. She opens her mouth in wisdom. . . . Her children rise up and bless her; Her husband also, and he praises her. . . ."

Ugh. This is not someone you'd want as a next-door neighbor. Let's face it; my kids do not rise up and call me blessed. Most days they just rise up and call me.

But then I realized that this passage doesn't describe this woman's "to do" list for a day; it describes what she's accomplished in her whole life.

"There is an appointed time for everything," wrote the author of Ecclesiastes. "And there is a time for every event under heaven."[2] In a woman's life, there are different seasons. There is time for a career, time to have babies, time to drive carpools, time to worry over teenagers, time for "empty nests" (and for second honeymoons), time for grandchildren, time for taking care of our own parents. There is time for a spotless house, time for gardening, time for getting degrees and for volunteering and teaching a Sunday School class. And there is time for cooking, for laundry, for reading, taking walks, and going out to dinner. But these worthwhile pursuits simply can't happen all at once. Each season has its rewards and blessings, its struggles and pain. And each is only a season. The trick is to learn to say "What time is it?" and to let go of the things there is no time for right now.

TO BE IS TO DO

The hot item around my neighborhood is a calendar of humorous daily thoughts called "Women Who Do Too Much." We are a veritable bouquet of busyness on our cul-de-sac, a good cross-section of "seasons" in life.

Lynn is the PTA president this year; she's up at school more than her children are! She is a Volunteer with a capital V.

Vicky is a single mom with a teenage son and a full-time job. I see her on Saturdays, mowing and weeding and catching up around the house.

Sue has three kids, volunteers in the school clinic, and drives the swim-team carpool. She's my neighbor who bakes homemade cookies and always has an open door and a cup of coffee for you.

Kathy has a houseful of family from elementary to college age. She's always got a car full of equipment and a driveway full of various age kids, bikes, and cars. She's also our environmentalist, who recycles with a vengeance and grows organic vegetables.

Toni has teenage boys; she's always got a basketball game going in her backyard and burgers on the grill. She also mows everybody's lawn with her riding mower and carries out an incredible ministry through a neighborhood Bible study she's taught for years.

Karen has small children and works a couple of days a week at her husband's business.

Linda is a high-school teacher whose children are grown. She's a fantastic gardener and makes great peach preserves.

I'm the one with the new babies and the driveway full of Hot Wheels. Dennis is in the music business, which means we keep odd hours, sometimes work at home, and sometimes travel a lot. (In Nashville, there's a musician in almost every neighborhood. We provide the local color.)

Is your neighborhood anything like mine? Chances are, the "seasons" represented are as diverse as those on my street. The one thing we all have in common is that we are busy. Our schedules are full. Our lists are long.

HUMAN DOINGS

Claire wrote to me once that she thought we human beings ought to be called "human doings" instead! After all, that is how we identify ourselves—by what we do, what we get done.

The great thing about heaven, Claire said, is that we will finally have the time just to be. There'll be time to sit together, to talk, to sing one more chorus of our favorite hymn, with all the harmonies. Best of all, we'll have time just to be with Jesus, to sit with him for as long as we like. Maybe that's when we'll finally discover what we were meant to be all along.

When Jesus was on earth, I really don't think he kept a "to do" list. ("Heal blind man, 11:30; cast out demon, 2:15; Monday: stop by temple and rebuke Pharisees.") I think he just was who he was—and who he was, was God. God whose handshake could heal leprosy. God whose dinner conversation could reveal eternal secrets. God who let children sit on his lap. God who had an agenda, but always had time to stop for a miracle on the way.

If you want a funny picture of the contrast between Jesus and the "human doings" who followed him, read the Gospel of Mark straight through sometime. Mark is a fast-paced gospel, with one episode right after another and no commercials in between. Most of the time, the disciples seem to have their tongues hanging out, and it shows in their attitude. They come back from days of healing and teaching, get in a boat to go for a little retreat, and find five thousand people waiting for them on the other side of the lake. "Send them away," you hear them groan. And later, "Who's going to feed all these people, we'd like to know?"

By contrast, Jesus never seems rushed or harried. If his vacation is interrupted, he is willing to spend all day on the hillside. He is glad to stop on the road for a group of lepers or sit by the well in deep conversation with a woman nobody else will give the time of day. He senses when the crowd is getting hungry and takes measures to handle the situation. He picks up on the look in a man's eye when the question is crucial, hears the urgency in a voice when the situation is desperate. And while the others are sleeping in exhaustion, he is alone on the mountain praying.

And have you ever noticed that much of Jesus' ministry seemed to take place on the way to somewhere? So many stories in the gospels begin, "As He was going. . . ." or "While He was walking. . . ." Jesus didn't set out with a set "ministry agenda." He just got up and went through his day, and in the course of it, he was sensitive to those he encountered.

Jesus always knew what time it was. He was directed not by a list of things to do, but by his knowledge of who he was.

TOO MUCH "TO DO"

Do you have a "to do" list? I bet you do. You may carry it in a Daytimer, keep it on a monogrammed notepad, or scratch it on the back of an envelope. But most of us have a list of one kind or another. And our "to do" lists define us. ("I do, therefore I am.") At the end of the day, we like to cross items off and say, "I did that." The question is not, as Shakespeare put it, "To be, or not to be," but "to do, or to do even more."

A "to do" list can be a great tool, helping you focus on doing what is most important in your life. Or it can really tyrannize you. It can run your life. It can, at times, be a great source of guilt, if you don't get it all done.

I've become quite skilled at making "to do" lists; you might say I've graduated to the advanced level of list making. I now have "A" lists, "B" lists, and "C" lists of things to do. (Did you know there are actually methods available to help you organize your "to do" list?) I can prioritize and procrastinate with the best of them. See, I can justify not getting a "C" thing done today by simply moving it to the "B" list tomorrow.

To be fair, there are things on my list that are very important—like clean underwear, or the chapter that is due to my editor next week. I really should get those things done.

But there are also some truly important things that don't usually show up on my list—like having coffee with the friend who drops by or inspecting a new crop of toadstools down under the bridge with my small son. These are things I should do, too, in spite of what doesn't get crossed off on my list at the end of the day.

THE MINISTRY OF INTERRUPTION

For those of you who find yourself enslaved to your "to do" list, let me offer you a way of looking at your day that can offer you some of Jesus' grace and his freedom to be. It's called "the ministry of interruption." My friend Katharine Bryan, who works for the Tennessee Baptist Convention, taught me this. Here's how it works:

First, I write down my "to do" list for the day. It looks something like this:

1. Grocery shopping
2. Wash whites
3. Call committee members re Tues. meeting
4. Mail electric and water bills
5. Seth: soccer practice 4:00
6. Bake brownies for PTA open house
7. Run errands

Next, I start out that morning by making my grocery list and putting in a load of laundry. Then I sit down to make committee phone calls. "Call waiting" interrupts me, and I take the call, which is from the school nurse. My neighbor's son, Josh, threw up in second period. Karen is not home, and my name is on her emergency list. Can I come and get Josh?

I bring Josh home, make him a bed on the sofa, and take his temperature. I leave a message for his mom. Then I spend the day caring for Josh, finishing the laundry, and making my phone calls.

Karen comes home at three o'clock, horrified to find that I've had her son all day. She gratefully takes him home. My own kids come home shortly after that; I throw them in the car and head out for the grocery store, post office, and soccer practice.

On the way, I pass my friend Peggy's kids walking by the side of the road, crying. I stop. Their dog has run away; they're looking for him. Also, they forgot their house key, and they're locked out. Now, Peggy's a single mom; she won't be home from work until six o'clock. In late November in Nashville, it will be cold and dark outside by five o'clock.)

So I pile the kids in the car and drive around looking for their dog. Then I take the kids home with me and call Peggy to let her know I've got them.

It's too late for soccer, and there's no sign of the dog. To cheer everyone up, I bake the brownies that were meant for the PTA. I throw together dinner with what I have in the fridge, since I never got groceries. My husband comes home, Peggy comes to get her kids. The day is shot.

Now, here's what I see when I finally get back to my "to do" list:

1. Grocery shopping
2. Wash whites
3. Call committee members re Tues meeting
4. Mail electric and water bills
5. Seth: soccer practice 4:00
6. Bake brownies for PTA open house
7. Run errands

Just looking at the list, it appears that I got almost nothing done today, doesn't it? I guarantee that my neighbors Karen and Peggy both think I did something important!

So here's how I handle my list. I add these items to the bottom of it, then cross them off:

8. Help Karen by taking care of sick child all day
9. Look for lost dog
10. Rescue Peggy in emergency
11. Bake brownies for kids

Wow! I actually had a busy day. And I did some very important things—very important in the lives of two other women and their families. I'm amazed that I also managed to do three loads of laundry and make my committee calls. So instead of feeling like a failure, I give myself a pat on the back! I'm pretty super!

GOD IN OUR OWN IMAGE

See, it's all a matter of perspective. Our perspective tends to be, "What am I going to do today?" But God's perspective is "Who are you going to be today?" Our concern is quantity—how many things we can cross off our list. His concern is quality—the eternal significance of what we did with each moment.

My friend Gloria Gaither says we are all created exactly equal in one way: we all have twenty-four hours in a day. Our challenge comes in how we spend what we've been given. And that's a tricky point, because what is often most important is not something you can put a check by and say, "I did that."

God's values are different from ours. We tend to be project-oriented, while he is people-oriented. We are reactive; He is reflective. We are interested in solutions; he is interested in salvation.

Somewhere along the line, we have gotten the wrong idea of God. We have made him over in our image; we've imposed our value system on him. He is not performance-oriented. He does not give grades. He does not keep permanent records, like some high-school guidance counselor. (It wasn't until I was about thirty that it dawned on me that my neighbors and employers for years to come were not going to know that I skipped fifth period in the tenth grade to sneak into the gym balcony and watch cheerleader tryouts.)

I saw a great T-shirt the other day. It said:

LET'S GET SOMETHING STRAIGHT:
(1) THERE IS A GOD.
(2) YOU'RE NOT HIM.

We sure try to be, though. We think we need to be all-knowing, all-seeing, possessing all the answers and able to handle whatever comes our way. We think of ourselves as some modern version of Cinderella's fairy godmother, showing up with a magic wand and a solution for every dilemma—bibbidy-bobbidy-boo, and everything's fixed.

I DO IT!

Rachel Farrell, the daughter of my friends Bob and Jane Farrell, had a fixation on magic wands when she was small. One Christmas she asked for a magic wand. They gave her a shiny plastic one, with glitter. She bopped a few things with it and caught on that it was just pretend.

So the next Christmas Rachel got more specific; she wanted a *real* magic wand (and don't try to fake me out again). Bob and Jane thought they were being real clever by giving Rachel a puppy with a note attached that said,

Dear Rachel:

I can't give you my magic wand. I need it. But here is a real puppy instead. I hope you like him.

Love, Santa

Well, she did like the puppy, but she also made it clear that he was not what she really wanted.

The third year, when the real magic wand again appeared on the list, Bob and Jane tried to reason with Rachel. Wouldn't she like some other things? Toys? Dolls?

"No," Rachel replied, "If I have a magic wand, I can make my own stuff."

That's what we want. We don't want to have to ask, even from God, who has a lot more resources than Santa. We want to make our own stuff. We've become so competent at moving mountains and making things happen, we've left no room for Him to meet our needs.

(I have a theory that it's virtually impossible to have a whole lot of faith and also have credit cards. Who needs to wait on the Lord for something when you can get it now and pay on it in installments?)

We are like my two-year-old, whose standard response these days is, "No! *I* do it!" It doesn't matter whether or not he really can; most of the time he can't. Matt doesn't care. He just doesn't want to need any help. He wants to prove he is a Big Boy.

BE STILL AND KNOW

God has made it clear that we do not have to prove we are Big Girls. It is not our job to do it all; it isn't even within our power.

"I know the plans that I have for you," the Lord says to us.[3]

"Trust in the LORD with all your heart, And do not lean on your own understanding."[4] It is his job to have all the answers; it's our job to ask the questions.

"My God shall supply all your needs."[5] It is his role to provide. Our role is to need.

When our son Seth was little, he had a pair of Superman pajamas, complete with a red flannel cape and a big *S* on the chest. Every night after his bath, he would put on those "jammies," climb up on the back of the sofa, flap his cape, and jump off. He was just sure he could fly. After all, he had the cape; he had the outfit. He'd seen the guy do it on TV. If he just tried hard enough, he could be Superman, too.

We finally had to break the news to him that there is no Superman. Somebody just made him up. No matter how hard he flapped his cape, he wasn't going to fly.

I know we must look like that to God at times—flapping our capes, trying so hard. "Give it up," he must want to say to us. In fact, he has said that to us. He has said, "Be still and know that I am God."

Only one Person has the power to do it all. Only one Person has the strength we keep trying to muster, the control over time we think we possess. Only one Person can meet everybody's needs, has all the answers.

Be still, he says, and know who I am. Let me show you what's important to do and what's not. Let me tell you what time it is. Let me help you with the things you're not good at. It's okay to be weak; I am strong. It's okay to be tired; lean on me!

I have news for you: Superwoman is a myth. I don't care if you have seen her on TV or in a magazine. Somebody made her up. She doesn't exist, and you can't be her. You're just a normal woman with the same twenty-four hours as everybody else. You have your good days and your bad days. Sometimes you do it all beautifully; sometimes you don't. And don't kid yourself—it's just the same for all the rest of us. We aren't doing it all, either, no matter how hard we seem to be flapping our capes.

Hey, you, with the *S* on your chest: I've got an idea. Why don't we all climb down off the back of the sofa and sit down together with a cup of coffee? I'm willing to ignore something on my "to do" list, if you are.

Come to Me,
all who are weary and heavy-laden,
and I will give you rest.
Take My yoke upon you,
and learn from Me,
for I am gentle and humble in heart;
and YOU SHALL FIND REST FOR YOUR SOULS.
For My yoke is easy, and My load is light.

MATTHEW 11:28–30 NASB

Surrender Your "To Do" List

Today, make a conscious effort to surrender
your time and energy to God's priorities.
Pray over your schedule, your list of things to do.
Ask God to show you how he wants you
to spend your time today.
Then, keep your eyes open for the opportunities
he brings your way for the "ministry of interruption"!

❦

Father, you are the author of time. Your timing is perfect.
And when I find myself rushed and stressed,
I know it's because I am not listening to you.
Show me how to spend my hours, my days.
Free me from the tyranny of my "to do" list.
Open my eyes and ears to the opportunities
you bring into my path,
and help me to be willing to be interrupted
by your presence.

AMEN

SIX

Once Upon a Romance

Claire's chapter about marriages that weren't made in Hollywood

How many cups of coffee,
how many dreams we've shared?
How many funny moments,
how many problems and how many prayers?
Have I mentioned it to you lately,
you're still the one I need,
the one that I love and lean on,
the one that I turn to, the one I believe.

What would I do without you?
Where would I be without you and me?
You're so much a part of each beat of my heart,
for God has made one out of two,
and what would I do without you?

How many mortgage payments,
how many skates and bikes?
How many ways we've struggled,
how many kisses after the fights?
Looking across tomorrow,
we've got no guarantees,
but I know we'll be together,
still finding our answers down on our knees.

What would I do without you?
Where would I be without you and me?
You're so much a part of each beat of my heart,
for God has made one out of two,
and what would I do without you?

CLAIRE CLONINGER[1]

*S*ix weeks ago, at 3:22 A.M., I got a call from our now twenty-one-year-old Andy. Not so many years ago, a middle-of-the night call from Andy would have automatically meant bad news. But those days—thank you, Lord—are past. And this news was anything but bad.

"Hurro," I muttered thickly into the receiver.

"Mom? Is that you?"

"Yes, I think so," I answered sleepily.

"What're you doin'?" he inquired (a little inappropriately, I thought).

"Andy," I growled, squinting one bloodshot eye at the neon dial of the bedside clock, "It's three-twenty-two in the morning. What do you think I'm doing? I'm sleeping. Or, at least I was. . . . What are you doing?"

"Mom," he said, excitedly, "I just got up off my knee from asking the foxy and adorable Jenni Uplinger to be my bride. And the foxy and adorable Jenni Uplinger has just responded in the affirmative."

"Oh, Andy!" I gushed, all hostility at being awakened suddenly gone. We dearly love Andy's Jenni, and to tell the truth, I was not overly surprised. He had been asking an awful lot of questions lately about "how to know that you know that you know she's the one."

"Jenni wants to talk to you, okay?"

"Put her on," I answered.

"Mrs. Cloninger," said the sweet, young voice on the other end. (Since that night, I've been encouraging her to call me "Claire," and she has been trying her hardest.)

"Hi, Jenni," I responded.

"Mrs. Cloninger," she said again, "Andy told me that you've been praying for his wife-to-be ever since he was a little boy."

"That's right. I have."

"Well, I guess you didn't know who you were praying for all those years. And I sure didn't know there was someone praying for me. But now that I do know, I'd like to thank that someone."

Tears filled my eyes. The answer to my prayer was calling to thank me for praying! Oh God, you are so awesome!

I still haven't totally recovered from Andy and Jenni's late night call. Ever since I hung up the phone, I've been drifting from room to room in a giddy and romantic state of mind. (This is not a hard accomplishment for me.)

I've also found myself doing a lot of reminiscing—looking back through the beginnings of our own marriage, which is heading toward its thirty-year anniversary this February. In my mind, I've been going over all the feelings and events that have brought us this far.

But I've been doing more than reminiscing. To tell the truth, I think I've been looking for something—some harvest of wisdom from lo, these many decades—something weighty and profound that I could pass on to my son and my new daughter (should it ever occur to them to ask for such a thing). Considering how much time has elapsed since I first dreamed of being a bride, I can't help thinking that surely I must have learned a little something!

SEEKING THE FAIRY-TALE SCENARIO

If there is one area of life in which most of us yearn for a fairy-tale scenario—and if there is one area of life in which our expectations get totally out of line with reality—it's in the area of love and marriage. Little girls especially learn to look for the arrival of the "one and only" the way a drowning man looks for a boat. By the time we're of dating age, most of us have watched a million movies that conclude with the scene where the boy gets the girl. (Rarely do we get to see this same couple fifteen years later when he's lost his job and his hair and she's having an identity crisis and the oldest child has just entered adolescence!)

Like most little girls, I fantasized about having a fairy-tale wedding. My sister, Ann, and I had a costume trunk at the foot of our bed from which we could pull together authentic-looking bridal regalia in a matter of seconds. I had made hundreds of "play like" trips down the aisle by the time I decided to go for the real thing.

Like most little girls, too, I had focused the greatest part of my attention on the wedding and little or none at all on the marriage. Living with someone through good and bad 'til death-do-us-part were words in a game of make-believe, not the kind of commitment I was in any way prepared to make back then.

I don't guess anybody comes onto this planet naturally equipped with the unselfish kind of love required for a happy marriage. I certainly didn't. I arrived with a "what's in it for me" attitude. (I believe this is what is known as the fallen condition of humanity!)

My parents raised me to share my toys and be kind to the new girl at school and put part of my allowance in the collection plate on Sunday. A generous spirit did not come naturally, but by the time I was old enough to date I had acquired an exterior which was sufficiently civilized to gain entrance into many social situations and most public places. Underneath the polite exterior, however, I was still very much out for number one.

I sincerely believed that what I wanted was to fall madly in love with this perfect person and live for him and him only. I couldn't wait to share my all with him and make him happy for the rest of his life. (I didn't know it at the time, but what I really wanted under that facade of self-sacrifice was to have this perfect person live for me and me only, share his all with me, and make *me* happy for the rest of my life!)

What I was waiting for, by and large, was this larger-than-life, idyllic Hollywood romance to materialize out of nowhere, thereby eradicating boredom, bad news, depression, heartburn, hangnails, and other assorted negative stuff. I fully believed a prince had been dispatched in my general direction. It was only a matter of time. My foot was all poised and ready for the glass slipper.

A PRINCE NAMED "SPIKE"

But instead I fell in love with Spike.

Spike is not his real name. His real name is Robert Arrington Cloninger. He is named for his father, Robert, and his maternal grandmother, whose maiden name was Arrington. To me the name is strong yet sensitive, down-to-earth yet ethereal, practical yet beautiful. Unfortunately, however, he has never been called Robert Arrington, or even Robert, even in passing. When he was an infant in arms, one of his uncles dubbed him "Spike," and the name stuck.

I've always known Spike. Long before I entered kindergarten, Spike was at most of the birthday parties I attended. His parents and my parents were friends. His best friend, Danny, was my next-door-neighbor, so Spike was always in our backyard, or so it seemed. He was part of the neighborhood scene, a familiar character in the drama of my childhood.

Spike taught my little brothers to shoot basketball. When I was fourteen, he and Danny taught me to water ski. (They simply wouldn't let me back in the boat until I managed to get up on the skis!) Spike and I performed together in our elementary-school chorus production of *H.M.S. Pinafore*, and in high school we sang a duet entitled "Pretty Baby" in the Key Club Minstrel.

Though we had a few dates back in those days, they were not of the romantic variety. In fact, we were such chums to each other that neither of us even considered these outings a "date."

Usually Spike would call at the last minute and say something like, "I can't get a date for tomorrow. You wanna go out?" As unflattering as that type of invitation might sound to you, it didn't wound or surprise me one bit. After all, this was my old buddy, Spike.

So, if anyone back then had told me I'd be marrying Spike Cloninger some day, I would have been pretty disappointed. I was on the lookout for somebody tall, dark, and mysterious who would sweep into my life one day and carry me off into that distant and romantic locale known as "happily ever after." Instead Spike (who was tall, dark, and anything but mysterious) came home from the Army one summer so handsome and grown up and comfortably dear that I fell for him in spite of myself.

I married Spike in the middle of my junior year at Louisiana State University. We knew we'd have only three months to live together as married people before he'd have to go overseas for thirteen months—without me. It was a less-than-optimal situation for newlyweds. But we were so blissful (and, let's face it, so ignorant) that it seemed like an almost romantic dilemma. So I quit school and we rushed headlong into the big middle of it.

We married in February and moved immediately to Ft. Knox, Kentucky. There we had three fun-filled months during which he learned to be an armor commander and I learned the difference between paprika and chili powder.

Then, the next thing we knew, he was leaving for what the Army called a "hardship tour" in Korea. And I was moving home to Louisiana to live with Mom and Dad for thirteen months—which turned out to be something of a hardship tour in itself.

Not that Mom and Dad weren't great. But Mom described my life that year pretty accurately when she said that I had become a "swoose"—that is to say, not a swan and not a goose. I didn't fit in with my single friends since I wasn't single. And I didn't fit in with the few married couples my age that I knew, since the other half of my "couple" was on the other side of the globe.

Spike's homecoming thirteen months later was very exciting but also very difficult for both of us. Here we were, sixteen months into this marriage, but we had actually lived together only three short months. Here we were, supposed to know each other so well, when actually we had both changed dramatically during the thirteen months we had been apart. Here we were, one flesh, but feeling more like total strangers.

I really struggled that first year after Spike's return. He was extremely busy with his Army responsibilities, and I was in a new place without any family or friends for the first time in my life. I didn't know how to talk to him about what I was going through or what I needed, and I'm sure I wasn't much good at listening for his needs either.

What's more, I felt guilty about not being happy. I know that probably sounds dumb, but I was certain it was something I was doing wrong. Newlyweds were supposed to feel all "glowy" and perfect, but I was feeling mostly lonely and confused. What was wrong with me?

All the childhood games I had played dressing up in a white veil and carrying a bouquet had not prepared me for the realities of making a life with another human being. All the bride magazines I had read about having the picture-perfect ceremony and reception had neglected to mention what happens after the guests go home.

NOT A HAPPENING, BUT A DISCIPLINE

I may have been more naive than many people, but I don't really think my story is that unusual. Most people are not really prepared for marriage or what it will be like. Lots of us have one kind of person in mind and end up marrying another. And others walk down the aisle with what they assume to be "the person of their dreams," only to discover, months or years into the marriage, that their perfect dream of a partner has acquired some of the elements of a nightmare!

More often than not the dream marriage (like the dream partner) will run into its nightmare moments, as well. There will be unexpected adjustments to be made—unplanned-for bumps and disagreements and areas of conflict. I don't know anyone who has been married any length of time at all who would describe marriage as a totally smooth sail into the sunset of their expectations. It's not a picnic. Or, as Calvin Miller once said, it's "not a happening, but a discipline."[2]

And yet, despite the fact that our romance and marriage has not exactly followed the "glass slipper scenario"—despite the fact that it has had more real life to it than fairy tale—I wouldn't have missed being married to Spike Cloninger for the world. This marriage is where I've grown up. It's where I've found my faith. It's been the sandpaper the Lord has used to rub the rough edges off of us both and make us into more of what he had in mind for us as individuals. And with some of the rough edges off, after nearly three decades, we finally do fit together as one.

A MAJOR HURDLE TO ONENESS

Arriving at "oneness" doesn't happen without getting over some hurdles. One of the major hurdles to oneness that I observe in marriages is that each partner brings with him or her the history, the experiences, the values, the prejudices, the temperaments of other lives. When two people marry, their parents and grandparents inevitably get into the act.

Look back with me at our families of origin, and you'll see what I mean. (Don't worry; I didn't bring the family slides!)

I grew up in a frame house on a shady street with two parents and four siblings. My mama, Virginia, was an only child, raised by an alcoholic father and a highly emotional mother. Mom is artistic, introverted, perceptive, intelligent, sensitive, shy, and loving. She can be pensive and sometimes melancholy. She has a great sense of humor.

Charlie, my dad, was the oldest of two boys from his father's first marriage. His mother died of pneumonia when Dad was five, so he was raised by an aunt and uncle in a small town. Somewhere in those bumpy and unstable years, Dad decided it would be a good idea always to try looking on the bright side. He is an extrovert—practical, energetic, action-oriented, and stubbornly optimistic. He's a good listener and a good friend.

Mama's family, the Wheadons and Kilpatricks, were from north Louisiana. They were English and Scotch-Irish. Dad's family, the deGravelles, were from the French area of south Louisiana (which might as well be a different country!)

Spike's parents, Marjorie and "Dobbin" (yes, his name was Robert, too), were from a little town in North Texas named Electra. Marjorie was a delightful combination of the personalities of her parents. (Her mom was a dreamer and her father was a practical and pragmatic man's man.) Marjorie was raised to believe that everything was possible, and she invariably proved that to be true. A five-foot-tall dynamo, sunny and outgoing, Marjorie never met a stranger. She was strong and compassionate and sometimes blind to the faults of those she loved.

Dobbin was from a family of ten children. His father was one of those big, tough, thoroughly masculine Texans who would rough and tumble and tease the grandchildren mercilessly. I never heard Dobbin's mother, Effie, say a single word. (After raising ten children, no wonder. She was probably just plain worn out!) She wore simple cotton housedresses and her hair in a knot and was usually doing some kind of handwork while everyone else was talking.

I often wondered how Dobbin, raised by shy, retiring Effie, adjusted to his bubbling, outgoing bride, but he did. Dobbin was kind, romantic, stubborn, gentle, and one of the humblest men I've ever known.

The above paragraphs list just a few facts about my parents and Spike's, which I've reported succinctly and rather unemotionally. But these are not unemotional facts. They are the components of four unique, specific individuals, our parents. They are the raw ingredients of their two marriages as well as the components which were programmed into our own.

And so, even though it seemed in the beginning that our marriage (Spike's and mine) was a combination of only two lives, we gradually discovered that it was actually a combination of many lives. Because of this, when we began to relate to each other as husband and wife, we sometimes found that the conflicts in our marriage were not actually between the two of us as individuals. They were, instead, a clash between some hand-me-down preference of his family's and some inherited idea from mine!

I started married life with the naive assumption that our life together was like an empty suitcase which we would pack with all the beautiful treasures that love would lead us to discover. In actuality, we arrived on our honeymoon with a lot of extra baggage already packed full of beliefs and traits and tendencies we acquired from our families. The challenge in our marriage has been in the careful unpacking of each other's bags—delighting in some of the wonderful things that we find in each other, making peace with others, and making a joint decision to throw a few things overboard!

Jenni and Andy, too, will arrive on their honeymoon with "extra baggage" and emotional "heirlooms"—some from Jenni's family, and some from ours. And they will spend their lifetime together as man and wife unpacking the treasures and the white elephants of each other's personalities—polishing and appreciating, reupholstering and rearranging, and making a comfortable blend of all the traits and qualities they'll learn to treasure in each other.

I wish I knew some magic formula for making the process of "unpacking their lives" a totally painless process. If such a formula were in my possession, I would already have patented it—and be rolling in dough! Unfortunately, as far as I know, such a formula doesn't exist.

But I have actually gleaned a kernel or two of insight in these twenty-nine years. I have managed to replace some of my flowery expectations and misconceptions with enough wisdom and reality to help keep our boat afloat. And these I bequeath to you, Andy and Jenni, free of charge.

(Come to think of it, maybe all mothers-in-law should write a marriage chapter containing every bit of advice they'd ever want to give their kids, neatly typed and double-spaced. Then, instead of butting in with lots of verbiage and helpful hints, she could just calmly suggest "page seven, paragraph three" and shut up!)

KERNELS OF INSIGHT

What did I think I was getting myself into that long-ago Saturday morning, 23 February 1963, when I took my dad's arm and walked down the long, polished center aisle of the Episcopal church to link my life with Spike Cloninger's? What did I believe and hope and expect my marriage to be that it has not been? And what has it been that I never expected?

Misconception #1: The Degree of Difficulty Theory

To begin with, I thought marriage would be easier. I thought we'd fit together more or less automatically, like Barbie and Ken. I thought love would glide us through the "bonding process" without a hitch. Or, at the very least, I thought that any struggles would simply take on the romantic sheen of a classy melodrama in which we had been cast as the romantic leads.

But I have found that very little seems to happen automatically in a marriage relationship. Marriage is work—sometimes gritty, sweaty, uncomfortable work. In fact, I figure that the degree of difficulty in combining two lives ranks somewhere between rerouting a hurricane and finding a parking place in downtown Manhattan.

I am of the opinion that only God himself can make a marriage happen really well. And when he does it his way, it's one of his very best miracles. I mean, the Red Sea was good, but for my money this is better. What God can create out of the combined ingredients of two surrendered lives is indeed "infinitely more than we ever dare to ask or imagine."[3]

Misconception #2: The Clairvoyant Spouse Theory

When I was a newlywed, I thought that if Spike really loved me, he should be clairvoyant (or at least Claire-voyant!). He should automatically *know* what I was thinking and feeling and what I needed without my verbalizing a thing. So if my needs weren't being met exactly as I felt they should be, I would jump to the conclusion that he didn't love me.

It was an enormous breakthrough for me to realize that Spike really wanted to be there for me. He wanted to be able to meet my needs the best he could. But he wasn't a mind-reader. He couldn't know what I needed unless I told him!

And so, over the years, we've gotten better and better at sharing our thoughts and feelings, clarifying our hopes, needs, and expectations for each other and our relationship. As a consequence, we've gotten better at meeting each other's needs and helping each other realize some of those hopes and expectations.

Misconception #3: The Key to Happiness Theory

Before I was married, I thought being happy meant getting what you want. I have learned, after twenty-nine years of marriage, that being happy means loving what you get.

Misconception #4: The Beef-Stew Theory

In the early years of our marriage, when we were both in school and working a couple of jobs and not seeing nearly enough of each other, I had the misconception that a marriage could survive that kind of benign neglect.

I've learned since then to believe what my friend Chris Kelly always says: that making a marriage is a lot like making a stew; it will only be as good as the ingredients you put into it. If you are not taking the time for long talks and long walks together, for special dinners and afternoons off, for laughter and romance and celebrating each other, your marriage is going to be a pale and watery dish indeed.

Misconceptions #5: The Major Moments Theory

I somehow assumed early on that the most important days in a marriage would be the anniversaries, the weddings, the Christmases, and the family reunions. I have found instead that the most important day in any marriage is today!

My dear friend Mr. George told me something when he was a very old man—something I've never forgotten.

"Claire," he said, "Don't wait to be happy. Don't put it off. Martha Lee and I were always going to take a fancy trip out to California when Bubby was through with college. We never made it to California."

He chuckled a little sadly, shaking his head. I imagine he was remembering her. And then he said, "Call up Spike right now. You two ought to go out and do something wonderful together . . . tonight!"

Misconception #6: The Grin and Bear It Theory

I've got to confess that I used to have this major misconception about God and marriage. I thought that if we did get stuck in a lousy marriage,

God wanted us to hang on by the skin of our teeth and simply gut it out until the bitter end. I was wrong about that—terribly wrong. That's not what God wants at all. He wants us to stay together, all right. But it's not enough just to gut it out. He wants us to stay and pray and work and keep loving. He wants us to hope and believe in what He can do in us. He wants us to give him all the time and space he needs to make that lousy marriage into something not just tolerable, but beautiful and brave and strong, something that will witness to his mercy and his life in this world.

I think he's saying something to married couples, if we could just hear him, "Don't settle for a bad marriage, or even a mediocre one. Don't lower your expectations. Raise them! Trust me! I'm still a God of miracles!"

OPEN LETTER TO A YOUNG COUPLE

Dear Andy and Jenni,

Well, there you have it—all the wisdom it took me twenty-nine years to put together. I can just hear you saying, "That's it??? Twenty-nine years, and she gives us 'The Beef Stew Theory'?"

Okay. Okay. So, cut me some slack. I'm still down here in the trenches trying to figure it out for myself!

That reminds me of a sign that Auntie Ann's friend, Susan, has on her desk. It says, "This is a test. It is only a test. If it were your actual life, you would have been given better instructions."

That's kind of how I feel about marriage. No one gives you five foolproof steps for assembling a lasting relationship. Yet you stand at the altar together wildly promising to love, cherish, honor, etc., till death do you part. Pretty scary stuff.

But somehow I'm not scared for you. I see you two together, and I have tremendous hope for the whole human race! I believe in you. But what's more important, I believe in God. He's the one who thought up this institution in the first place, and you're his children.

So step out in faith. His grace is the best map I can give you. This is your actual life. And you're gonna do great!

Love, Mom

Arise, my darling,
my beautiful one, and come with me.
See! The winter is past;
the rains are over and gone.
Flowers appear on the earth;
the season of singing has come,
the cooing of doves
is heard in our land.
The fig tree forms its early fruit;
the blossoming vines spread their fragrance.
Arise, come, my darling;
my beautiful one, come with me.

SONG OF SONGS 2:10–13 NIV

Celebrate Your Marriage

Make a date with your husband
for a special night of reminiscing. Cook his favorite meal.
(Go on, go for it—candles, linen napkins, the works!)
Get out your wedding album and spend time together
looking at those fresh young faces and remembering.
Or get out some old love letters and
read them to one another. Think about the people you were
when you fell in love. What were each of you hoping for?
What opinions, traits, and attitudes were packed
in your "suitcases" when you arrived on your honeymoon?
How have they changed, or how would you like
to see them change? Share your worst memory and your best.
Pray for each other. Congratulate each other
on coming this far together—even if you've only got
a few months of married life under your belt!
Now look ahead. Plan something fun
you can do together—soon!

Father, thank you for this man, just as he is.
Thank you for putting us together and bringing us this far.
Help us not to take each other for granted.
Give us the courage to share our heartaches and our joys,
the compassion to hold each other up and affirm each other.
Give us the strength to defend each other and, especially,
the grace to forgive each other. Help us to
raise our expectations and to look for your miracles
in our marriage. Keep us turning back to you through it all.

AMEN

SEVEN

Whistle While
You Work

Karla's chapter about
dirty socks—and other ministries
of motherhood

My friend Suzie—what a gal!
Been married twelve years to her childhood pal.
Got a baby who's three now, and one on the way.
You can imagine how she spends her day:

Down on her knees, teachin' ABC's,
and bein' a faithful wife;
Gettin' paid in kisses, and pictures of fishes—
what a wonderful life!

And that's the way we praise him:
by the things we do and say.
Old men and children,
young men and maidens everyday.
It's a single, simple secret
that unlocks the universe:
that it's in the very ordinary,
putting him first—
that's the way that we praise him,
that's the way that we praise him.

KARLA WORLEY[1]

I *have a friend* who is a real shoe-aholic. She has a whole closet full of just shoes. No kidding. I thought that maybe when Imelda Marcos got into so much trouble for all her shoes, Jan might get some help with her addiction. Apparently not.

This is a woman who, if she has an outfit that is aqua and purple, has not just a pair of purple shoes, or a pair of aqua shoes, but a specific pair of purple and aqua shoes just for this outfit. And—I swear to you— they're all pumps. This girl wears pumps with jeans—casual pumps, of course. I did see her once, by the swimming pool, in a pair of sandals, but (you guessed it) they were high-heeled.

I remember pumps. I used to wear them back when I was a woman, before I became a mom. I used to dress for the office every morning and go out into the world in a pair of power pumps. But again, that was back before I had kids. Before I chased two-year-olds down the grocery store aisle, before I hauled diaper bags and strollers with me everywhere I went, before I served as a volunteer in the school clinic every Thursday, before I spent every afternoon at the soccer field. When I was a woman, I dressed as a woman.

Now I am a mother, and I have put away womanly things. Now I wear sneakers.

I have lots of sneakers. I have summer sneakers and winter sneakers, sneakers that lace and sneakers that slip on, leather sneakers and canvas sneakers. I have an entire wardrobe (but *not* an entire closetful!) of sneakers. Sneakers are a mother's best choice for shoes. We have to be ready for anything. We have to be surefooted, on our toes, keeping our balance while all about us is chaos. We're on our feet a lot. And, quite often, we "step in it."

That's a Texas phrase: "step in it." Do you know what it means? Texas is cattle country—lots of open range, lots of what we call "cow patties." So when you go out walking in Texas, you have to be careful that you don't "step in it."

Moms live the same kind of life; there's a lot of "it" around to step in. That's why we don't wear pumps a lot. You get my drift.

The ideal shoes for a mom should probably also have wheels, sort of like the ones waitresses wear at the old drive-in burger joints. Or maybe, even better, her feet should come equipped with wheels in the first place. She should also come with an extra pair of arms, a computerized memory bank, a two- or three-track mind, a big heart, lots of pockets, a built-in Kleenex dispenser. And she should be completely wash-n-wear. That'd be great.

MY MOTHER, MY SERVANT

Let's face it, motherhood is demanding. And don't let anybody kid you. Sure, you can be a mother and still do other things, but you can never do them quite as single-mindedly as you did them before. Motherhood takes over your life; it seeps into your work place, invades your personhood, makes over your figure and your wardrobe, wreaks havoc on your pocketbook, and completely devastates your Daytimer. Whether your kids are at home or at school or at daycare or with a babysitter, you are still their mother. You are their mother when they are awake or asleep—even when you're trying to sleep. You are their mother, and they are not about to let you forget it.

Nevertheless, motherhood has been good for me. It has made me a less selfish, less me-preoccupied person. More than anything else in my life, motherhood has helped me to understand the kingdom principle of servanthood.

Now, I've never really had a problem with the idea of serving Christ the King. That kind of servanthood is really kind of appealing. Picture it . . . the beautiful courts, the golden throne, the royal Master. Knowing that the reward for your service is to hear, "Well done, good and faithful servant."[2]

Serving a King is a privilege and an honor. It's serving his less-than-royal subjects that tends to stick in my craw. But that's exactly the people Jesus told us to serve! He said to his disciples,

> You know that those who are recognized as rulers of the Gentiles lord it over them; and their great men exercise authority over them. But it is not so among you, but whoever wishes to become great among you shall be your servant; and whoever wishes to be first among you shall

be slave of all. For even the Son of Man did not come to be served, but to serve, and to give His life a ransom for many.[3]

My children are the chalkboard upon which God is teaching me Christ's example of serving. And it's not always easy. Let's face it, these small people God would have me serve are, for the most part, whiny, messy, demanding, inconvenient, quirky, moody, and usually less than grateful. They take up a lot of my time and always seem to track mud on my clean kitchen floor. They don't act very royal, and they hardly ever say, "Well done, good and faithful mom." So it's hard at times to find it inspiring to serve them.

And yet Jesus said, "Inasmuch as you did it to one of the least of these My brethren, you did it to Me."[4] He really does count our serving these very ordinary humans as service unto the King.

A SOCK IN MY PURSE

I once went to a women's conference. (That's quite a statement in itself. If you knew me better, you would know that one of the things I try hardest to avoid in life is organized groups of church women!) Anyway, I went, and I heard a woman speak on the subject of servanthood. She said she used to view taking care of her husband and kids as drudgery, but then she asked God to change her attitude.

"Now," she said, "each time I pick up my husband or child's dirty sock off the floor, I use it as an opportunity to praise God for them."

All the women in the audience nodded and whispered, "Amen." I looked around and thought, "Am I the only one here who just doesn't get it?"

I felt so guilty that for a while I even carried one of my husband's socks around in my purse to encourage me! But I have to be honest with you and tell you that, while I am very thankful for my husband and my children, I have never thanked God that I had to pick up their socks!

The problem with being a servant-mother is that the job is just so ordinary. It's so day-to-day, so bread-and-butter, meat-and-potatoes. It's not very flashy. You spend all day washing, folding, and putting away clothes for your kids, and what do they do? They wear them and get them dirty again. You slave over a hot stove; they run in and eat and leave you to clean it up and cook some more. You sweep the dirt out; they track the dirt in. You make up the bed; they mess up the bed. The process just keeps going 'round and 'round in the same circle.

A carpenter or a gardener or even a garbage man can look back at the end of the workday and see a finished roof, a newly planted bed, a neighborhood cleaned and orderly. A mom looks back and sees the same stuff to do all over again. There's no monument to her hard work, no sense of an end to the job, no moving on to the next assignment. It's what my grandmother used to call "sweeping the same dirt."

But don't confuse ordinary with unimportant. Jesus didn't. He used ordinary, common elements of everyday life to teach great truths about the Kingdom: bread, water, fish, stones, stuff that everybody could understand.

Jesus spent the first thirty years of his life doing the ordinary work of a carpenter, living and working with his family. The years of his ministry were spent with ordinary people—eating with them, staying in their homes, letting their children sit on his lap. Ordinary, in Jesus's eyes, has the potential to become eternal.

ME? A MISSIONARY?

This came home to me recently as I was having a conversation with a friend who is a former foreign missionary. Sandy and her husband worked in a small village in Africa for several years. I have always had such awe for missionaries like Sandy. I have always thought they must be spiritual giants—certainly nothing like you and me.

I asked Sandy what her days as a missionary were like. And I guess I expected her to speak of how she traveled by elephant into the jungle to teach Bible stories to small African children who lived in huts and wore rings in their noses. How she preached to medicine men, handed out tracts to the natives, dragged stones from the river bank to help build a new church in some remote village.

Instead, she told me she took care of her children, taught them their school lessons, did housework, grew vegetables, cooked meals, shopped in the nearby town, visited with the women in her village as their children played together, and helped with Vacation Bible School.

"Wait a minute!" I said. "That's the same stuff I do every day!" Except, of course, that the women in my neighborhood wear jeans and sneakers, and I drive ten minutes to shop, rather than the three hours she traveled to the nearest town every other week. Still, Sandy had gone halfway around the world, left her family and friends, and learned a new language, just to do the simple, ordinary tasks of wife, mother, and neighbor. But those simple, ordinary tasks, done in the name of Jesus Christ, had the power to change lives.

That same power is available to you and me. It's the same power that transformed a fisherman named Peter into a great preacher. The same power that fed five thousand with a little boy's lunch. The same power by which an ordinary meal of wine and bread became Christ's body and blood, the symbols of life-changing power.

You and I are called to pack the lunches, to set the table, to prepare the meal; and then we are to invite the Christ who makes these ordinary moments into places where sacred things happen.

They come at the most unexpected times. Your child sits by you on the swing and, in an ordinary conversation, shares something incredibly private and precious with you. Or in the car, when he pipes up from the back seat and asks you where babies come from. Or tucking her into bed, when she asks you what heaven is like. These are moments you can't plan; you have to be there for them. The only way to catch them is to be there for all the other dull, ordinary, uneventful moments, too, because the really rare ones hide among the everyday and pop out at you when you least expect them.

Christ was born in a stable . . . perhaps to show us that there is no place, no thing so secular that it cannot be made sacred by his presence. A cup of water on a hot afternoon, a Band-aid on a finger, a clean bed, a home-cooked meal—these are our offerings to the King, and they are pleasing to Him. "Inasmuch as you did it to the least of these. . . ."

JUST DO IT

On a good day, when I've had my quiet time, when I feel close to God, when I'm in great spiritual shape, I know these things. On those days, mothering is a calling, a ministry. But most days, in the thick of the battle, my mind is not on spiritual things. Those are the days when I'm just trying not to "step in it." And I suspect that you have those days, too.

I've come to the conclusion that there is just a certain aspect of the servant-mother role that is not going to be inspirational or glamorous or, for that matter, gratifying. It is just stuff that has to be done. It's part of the service. Sometimes servant-mothers have to get up in the morning and, as the Nike ad says, "just do it."

Not for the reward. Not for the gratitude. Not so the world will be a better place. Not because you'll be the "best Mom." Not because anybody will notice (because they probably won't). Just do it. A servant serves because that is what she is paid to do, or bound in some way to do.

You and I were bought with a price: Christ's life. We are in his debt, bound to him. That's what Paul meant when he called himself "a bond-servant of Jesus Christ" (Rom. 1:1 NKJV) We owe Christ our very lives. We could never repay him. But he has told us that what he requires of us is to serve him by serving others.

"Do you love me?" Jesus asked Peter. "Then feed my sheep."[5]

Just do it.

WHAT'S LEFT OF MY RIGHTS?

"But what about me?" you ask. This is the primal question of our generation, we baby boomers. We are very "me"-oriented people. "How will it help me to realize my potential? Will it make me happy?" It all boils down to "What's in it for me?"

Several years ago, about the time I had my second child, a whole slew of magazine articles appeared about female corporate executives who were choosing to "downshift" or even give up their careers in order to have babies. This, according to the magazines, was the new trend. Very in—the ultimate expression of a woman's freedom and power.

One article featured an interview with a forty-year-old vice president of a major corporation who was now going to work out of her home as a consultant so that she could, as she put it, "have the experience of motherhood." It was a part of herself that she felt she was now ready to "realize."

Well, I had to laugh. Boy, is that woman in for a change of perspective! I have yet to meet a baby who is at all interested in "realizing" his mother's needs! Most babies I know just want you to meet theirs. I bet that, by now, that woman has "realized" some parts of herself she was not quite ready for!

Yes, motherhood is fulfilling. Yes, it is rewarding. It is miraculous and wonderful. It is what I always wanted to do with my life, and what I would never exchange for all the careers in the world. *But* . . . motherhood is mostly not about fulfilling your own potential; it is about helping your children fulfill theirs. It is not about having your own needs met; it is about meeting everybody else's. It is not about what you get; it is more about what you give.

And that is another fundamental principle of the Kingdom: you must lose your life in order to find it. The greatest must be the least. The servant shall be the master. The first shall be last. Die so that you may live. Give and you receive. Surrender and you are truly free.

This is a mystery; it is difficult for us to understand. It is even more difficult to live out.

SURRENDER OR DIE

I'm not talking about some warm, fuzzy surrender of your life to God. I'm not talking about being a martyr. (Q: How many mothers does it take to change a light bulb? A: That's all right, dear, I'll just sit here in the dark.)

I'm talking about a very conscious, eyes-open, get-down-to-brass-tacks surrender:

Surrender of your body: pregnancy wreaks havoc on your figure, and getting up in the night can sap your energy and ruin your complexion.

Surrender of your calendar: your children's schedules are going to crowd yours.

Surrender of your priorities: some things you've always wanted to do are going to have to wait.

Surrender of your checkbook: there are some things you can't buy or do because large chunks of your family's budget are earmarked for nursery furniture, school clothes, or braces.

Surrender of your leisure: it won't be so easy for a while to go out to lunch or go to a movie.

Surrender of the twenty-four hours in your day: some things on your list won't get done because someone else needed your attention.

You can make your own list of what you have to surrender right now while you are raising children. What is it for you? Going back to school? Writing a book? Serving on a committee? Buying a new car? Taking a trip? Recovering the couch? Having a guest room? Getting your nails done? Taking a nap? Keeping a clean house? Sleeping through the night? Having any privacy?

These are real, everyday, personal invasions of your rights. Don't underestimate them. The mother who surrenders them—and you may have to get down on your knees several times a day to surrender them—finds a freedom and release from the "have to," "should have," "ought to be," "why can't I" rat race that can make you feel like a slave rather than a servant.

The mother who hasn't learned to surrender will find herself feeling defensive and unappreciated, her joy replaced by a feeling of futility, her life one long list of chores.

I know. I have been that mother. Some days, I still am.

SERVING IN LOVE

Jesus was our model for servanthood. He was constantly on call. People waited for him on mountainsides, congregated on seashores; they accosted him on the road and interrupted him on the way to the Temple. When he sat down to eat, a crowd always gathered. I am sure he understands why mothers of young children never seem to be able to have "quiet time" with him, because people interrupted his prayer times, too.

But Jesus seemed always to respond appropriately, with the right word or touch. He knew when to give people what they needed and when they needed to be rebuked for asking. He never responded out of frustration or weariness. He never said, "In a minute," or "Not now; I'm busy."

Why?

Because Jesus knew the value of people. He loved them, and that is why he served them—even when he knew they would be ungrateful or unbelieving or even one day betray him. He loved people even though he knew their weaknesses full well. Jesus had come to earth out of his Father's love for these people. He knew they were the whole point.

A TALE OF TWO SISTERS

The Bible gives us a beautiful illustration of the complete picture of serving in the story of two of Jesus' friends, Mary and Martha. These two sisters lived with their brother, Lazarus, and several times when Jesus came through their village, he stopped at their house as a guest. It must have been a place where Jesus felt loved and accepted, where he was welcomed and made comfortable among his friends.

On the occasion described in Luke 10:38–42, Jesus was a guest in their home, and Martha was knocking herself out to make sure everything was done just right. I can just see her, cooking on all burners in the kitchen, making the Jewish equivalent of a Sunday pot-roast dinner with all the trimmings, while her guests laughed and relaxed in the front parlor, including her sister Mary, who was not helping at all. The hotter it got in the kitchen, the more irritated Martha got. About her fifth trip into the dining room to set something on the table, she'd had enough.

"Lord, don't you care that I'm doing all the work, and Mary's just sitting here?" she complained. "Tell her to get up and help me!"

Jesus' reply has always surprised me.

"Martha, Martha," he answered. Can't you just hear the tone of his voice as he took her gently by the shoulders? "Mary has chosen the most important thing."

Now, I can tell you, as the one who would have been in the kitchen slamming pans around, that Jesus' answer wouldn't sit too well with me. Oh, fine. Well, if we all just sit in the parlor, who do you think is going to see that we eat? I think I'll just try that this next Thanksgiving, when all fifteen of my friends and relatives are sitting in front of the Cowboys game on TV. I think I'll just sit down with them and put my feet up, and when they all get hungry for turkey about three that afternoon, I'll say, "Well, I've chosen the most important thing." That'll go over nicely.

But I've got to keep in mind that Jesus wasn't belittling Martha's service. Martha's hospitality was one of the reasons he loved to come to her house. But Martha had a problem that you and I often have—a problem of perspective. She was so focused on the menu that she forgot who she was cooking it for. She was so preoccupied with the table setting that she forgot about who would sit there. While she was in the kitchen making gravy, Jesus Christ himself was a guest in her front parlor.

Jesus was reminding Martha that she had forgotten the importance of who she was serving.

I have trouble remembering that, too, especially during a 3:00 A.M feeding. Especially at six in the evening, when my boys take one look at the dinner I've slaved over and pronounce, "I don't like this." Especially when they get the stomach flu and throw up on me. When they're fighting in the back seat of the car, or when I pick up the fourth pair of dirty socks off the floor, I tend to forget just who it is that I'm serving.

I forget, until I sit down with them and read a book together. I forget, until I watch them through the kitchen window, playing in the backyard, and I marvel at their imaginations. I forget, until I hear Matt sing "The Wise Man Built His House Upon the Rock" or Seth brings me a picture he has drawn. Until they snuggle up to me, all clean and toasty after their baths. Until I stop being so busy and, instead, sit down and look and listen and marvel.

But when I do sit down, I remember who it is that I am serving. Then I remember how much I love them, and that that is the reason I serve them. And I understand why Jesus says, "This is the most important thing."

*Then the King will say to those on His right,
"Come, you who are blessed of My Father, inherit the kingdom
prepared for you from the foundation of the world.
For I was hungry, and you gave Me something to eat;
I was thirsty, and you gave Me drink;
I was a stranger, and you invited Me in;
naked, and you clothed Me;
I was sick, and you visited Me;
I was in prison, and you came to Me."
Then the righteous will answer Him, saying,
"Lord, when did we see You hungry, and feed You,
or thirsty, and give You drink?
And when did we see You a stranger,
and invite You in, or naked, and clothe You?
And when did we see You sick, or in prison,
and come to You?"
And the King will answer and say to them,
"Truly I say to you, to the extent that you did it to one of
these brothers of Mine, even the least of them,
you did it to Me."*

MATTHEW 25:34–40 NASB

Celebrate Serving

Do you have a "Red Plate" tradition at your house?
My sister-in-law gave us a red dinner plate with
"You're Special Today" inscribed around the edges,
and we use that plate as a way
to express special appreciation for each other.
People in our family are honored
with that red plate at their place on their birthday,
or when they make a hundred on a test,
or sometimes just when they need to feel loved.

Pick out a special plate at your house and start a tradition
of your own. Or, choose one person in your family and
do something extra special for him or her one day:
prepare a favorite food, tuck "You're special" notes
into clean laundry, give a day off from chores,
or put their picture up on the refrigerator
labeled "Family Member of the Day."
Think of your own ways to celebrate
the ones you take care of
every day and to remember why you serve them.

Jesus, thank you for your example of servanthood.
Thank you for loving people so much that
you even gave your life for us.
Help me to love the people I serve in the same way.
Help me to remember how important they are to you,
to see them as the blessings they are.
Help me to serve them as though I were serving you.

AMEN

EIGHT

Let Your Hair Down, Rapunzel

Claire's chapter about birthdays, moving, and other traumatic changes

First a hit, then a flop,
nothing ever stays on top.
Prices rise, hemlines drop,
something's in and then it's not.

Fashions come, fashions go.
First it's yes, then it's no.
Hairlines shrink, waistlines grow—
no such thing as status quo.

But the more things change, the more God stays the same.
Through it all his love will reign.
The more things change, the more he stays the same.
No one else can make that claim.

Something stops, something starts—
perfect love to broken hearts.
There you were, here you are.
Take a spill, touch a star.

What goes up must come down.
Find the sky, then hit the ground.
First you smile, next you frown.
Give it time to come around.

But the more things change, the more God stays the same.
Through it all his love will reign.
The more things change, the more he stays the same.
No one else can make that claim.

Like a wall, one that will never fall. . . .
like a fire, one that will not expire . . ..
like a wind, one that will never end . . .
the Great I Am will never change.

CLAIRE CLONINGER[1]

L *ast night*, in painstaking detail, I wrote out in my journal all the major stuff that's occurred in my life during the past year and a half. It took me more than an hour. A lot has happened—a lot of wonderful and surprising things. When I finished writing, I was exhausted. I read the whole thing over, and it looked pretty good. On paper.

Unfortunately, we do not live our lives on paper. We live our lives where the fact hits the feelings. And the fact is—it's been a year of changes. And the feeling is—traumatic.

To begin with, I turned fifty last month. Talk about traumatic! I went into a three-day decline over it. It's really not like me to overreact like this. I promise you, I've never gotten weird over a birthday before. People joked about thirty, and I joked back. But thirty was a piece of cake. (Actually, knowing me, it was probably several pieces of cake!)

Then I got the black balloon treatment at forty, and I acted offended. But I wasn't really. I mean, what did I care? Forty was great! I was busier and happier than I had ever been. Job great, kids great, marriage great.

But fifty? Fifty suddenly seemed like such a high number. I just never thought of connecting it in any personal way with myself. I remember when my mother was fifty. She was a perfectly beautiful, accomplished, and gracious . . . old person.

How did this gigantic milestone sneak up on me without my noticing? I couldn't help thinking about something Dave Barry once said about how the aging process "is a big, sleek jungle snake, swimming just around the bend in the River of Life. It swallows you so subtly, an inch at a time, so you barely notice the signs."[2]

I remembered, too, how Ian Bedloe, the hero of Anne Tyler's *Saint Maybe*, had always thought that old people were born that way—"that age was an individual trait like freckles or blond hair, and that it would never happen to him."[3]

Yes, I was definitely caught off guard. The day of my birthday, I kept going up to the mirror and giving myself a reality check. "Hi, I'm fifty," I'd say to myself, just to see how it felt. It didn't feel so good.

But it wasn't just "the birthday" that was shaking me up. There was also "the move," which had happened four months before the birthday. We moved out of the home in which we had raised our kids—the large and lovely family home we had lived in for nineteen of our twenty-nine years of marriage. We moved out of a home with sidewalks and neighbors . . . and closets. And we moved into a log cabin with less than a thousand square feet of living area, one tiny bathroom, no closets to speak of, and forget the neighbors and sidewalks.

Granted, we are surrounded by acres of woods, and we look out on a spectacular view of the river forty feet below. Granted, we are going to add on to the house eventually. Granted, we are living Spike's wildest and dearest dream. But the fact is, for me, it's a big, big change. And for me, the feeling is—well, traumatic.

And it's not just the birthday, and not just the move. It's also . . . "the wedding." Yes, our son Andy is now married to the foxy and adorable Jenni Uplinger. The wedding was beautiful and special and a real high point in my life. The girl is a dream of a daughter-in-law. I couldn't love her more if she were my own. (I know people say that sometimes, but I really mean it.) Still, the territory is unfamiliar. I mean, all of a sudden, I'm somebody's mother-in-law.

The fact is—it's a change. And the feeling is—traumatic.

But wait! There's more! ("Add to the beautiful Ginsu knives, the bamboo steamer, and now what would you pay?") It's not just the birthday, the move, and the wedding. It's also "the good-bye." Fourteen months ago, two of our best buddies in all the world left Alabama for South Carolina. (In fact, looking back on it, I see their departure as the event that seemed to trigger this whole domino effect of change.)

Laura was the friend I had confessed my whole life to. And she loved me anyway. Laura's husband, John, was our pastor and our pal, a key person in our family's spiritual journey. Sure, we were happy for them. It was a good move for their family. Sure, they are still our friends. They always will be. But they are three states away. Change . . . traumatic.

Yes, I'm afraid there is more. This morning, our oldest son, Curtis, got on a plane and flew off to be a missionary. I know, I know. This is good, great, even wonderful news. Haven't I prayed his whole life that he would grow up to love and serve the Lord?

So why did I lie across my bed after he said good-bye and cry for an hour? Because the fact was—you guessed it—that his leaving was a change on top of many other changes. And the feeling was—you guessed it again—traumatic. I mean, all of a sudden here I was, somebody's mother-in-law, half-a-century old, sitting in a very empty nest in the middle of nowhere, with no children, no closets, and no best friend!

THE UNCHANGEABLE FACT OF CHANGE

Somebody very wise once said that the only unchangeable thing about life is the fact that it is constantly changing. As much as I would like to hollow out a comfortable little niche and gather my loved ones around me and stay exactly where I am, I just cannot do that. This moment is moving past me even as I am living it. The people around me are growing up and growing old. The colors of the seasons are subtly shifting and changing right before my eyes. Styles and fads are in and out almost before I've had time to catch on to them. The music industry in which I work is in a constant state of flux. Our political leaders, our media heroes, our sports idols move through our lives in an endless parade of change. Our relationships with our parents, our children, our marriage partners are constantly entering new phases that require emotional adjustments. People we have learned to love and depend on are called away, and our lives seem at times to be filled with good-byes.

And the change that affects us is not limited to events outside ourselves. Inside, too, we are constantly being drawn to new and different horizons that need facing, new and fearful precipices that need crossing, new and challenging heights that need scaling.

Or as Sue Monk Kidd put it in her book, *When the Heart Waits,*

the life of the spirit is never static. We're born on one level, only to find some new struggle toward wholeness gestating within. That's the sacred intent of life, of God—to move us continuously toward growth, restoring the divine image imprinted on our soul.[4]

What the author is saying, in effect, is that God is constantly at war with our comfort zones. He never planned for us to burrow in and get too cozy while living life on planet earth. He's in the business of remaking us, and there's no way we're going to go through the process of change without a measure of dis-ease. It's not *supposed* to be comfortable.

I don't think I ever really understood that the discomfort of change is an inescapable part of life, especially life as a Christian. Somewhere in my childhood I got the idea that it was possible and even desirable for me to get more and more schooled in the way the world works and thus more and more settled and set and comfortable the older I got.

In fact, I actually believed on some level that maturity means getting so familiar with life and so adept at playing its games that it would gradually begin to fit me like a comfy, old pair of house shoes. I thought I'd eventually reach a place where I could breathe a deep sigh and say, "Oh, so this is how life works! Now I understand! Now I can settle back and just enjoy it."

But, surprise, surprise! Reality has never matched that expectation. It has always seemed to me that the minute I catch on to one thing and get really good at it, it's over, and all the expertise I gained is no longer needed.

I had just gotten a handle on grade school, for instance, when I had to move on to junior high. I had just figured out the inner workings of junior high when I was catapulted into high school. Senior year in high school was fantastic. I was on top of it. I was a big fish. Then, suddenly, my little pond was replaced by this tremendous ocean known as college, and I was furiously paddling to stay afloat and gasping for breath again.

It was the same with raising children. I recall the challenge of bringing home Curt, our first baby—juggling all the responsibilities of bathing and changing and feeding and especially the maddening colic hour when the little fellow screamed nonstop for what seemed an eternity. I remember I had just figured out how to ease the pain of the colic hour and rock him back to sleep when the colic vanished, never to return. My newly discovered coping mechanism was no longer required!

That's the way it seemed to be with each of my two children at each stage in their lives—infant, toddler, grade school, teenage. I would struggle desperately to learn the new territory and finally seem to master it, just in time to be thrown headlong into something new and unfamiliar.

The Bible gives us plenty of warning on this ever-changing, transient quality of life. It tells us that we, like Abraham, are "strangers" and "pilgrims," spiritual tent dwellers. It makes it clear that God never intended us to spend every ounce of our time and energy making ourselves more and more comfortable on this planet—that we're actually all on our way to some place entirely different.[5] But as with many other passages in the Bible, we ingest this information with a grain of salt and go about the business of our lives trying to obtain earthly security and avoid change every way that we can.

THE STELLA IN ME

The idea of resisting change reminds me of a lady I knew in the town where I was raised. Her name was Miss Stella, and she was the aunt of a friend of mine.

Miss Stella spent all of her energy constructing rigid and unchangeable patterns of living for herself and her poor husband. She evidently found some sense of comfort in the ritual quality of the life they shared. Miss Stella did the same thing at the same hour of the day on the same day of the week three hundred sixty-five days, fifty-two weeks a year. If a friend called her to go to lunch and it was her day for a manicure, she always refused; changing course was just too much for her. Her menus were the same week by week, and on Tuesday night, when she and her husband ate out in the same restaurant, they always ordered the same thing.

Like Rapunzel locked in a tower with no way out, Miss Stella lived in a world that was close, predictable, and confining. She had walled herself in and was afraid to let her hair down. And sadly, as Miss Stella got older, arthritis set in. The joints of her body became as brittle and inflexible as the habits and patterns into which her life had become cemented.

It would be easy for me to point a finger and criticize Miss Stella's rigid little life or to laugh at her inflexible nature. But I could never do that, because there is a little bit of Miss Stella in me. I get things the way I want them, and I don't want anybody coming in and making me change.

In the mid-eighties, for instance, I was part of a church that was very close to my idea of heaven. I loved the songs and the worship and the pastor and the sermons and the people and absolutely everything about it. At last I've found the perfect church, I thought. I'm home. This is it. Don't anybody change a thing!

One summer during those "golden" years, a group of us traveled to a "spiritual renewal conference" in North Carolina. In a gorgeous Smoky Mountain setting, we laughed and played together; we studied and prayed together; we celebrated our faith and our friendships. It was fantastic.

I particularly remember one cool, crisp morning that ten of us packed a picnic lunch and climbed to the top of a mountain where there was a grassy field known as a "bald." It looked exactly like the opening scene in *The Sound of Music.* The sky was amazingly blue with huge, fluffy cumulus clouds drifting overhead. All around us, as far as we could see, was the untouched beauty of God's world.

After running and jumping and acting as silly as children, we spread out our blanket and had lunch together. During lunch and for a long time afterward, we talked about the things each of us had gone through as children. There were some tears and some prayers.

That was when our friend Jan pulled out the grape juice and crackers she had secretly bought at the Seven-Eleven. There on top of that windy mountain, feeling so much a part of each other's lives, we shared the Lord's supper.

What an incredible day! Before the sunlight began to fade, Spike set his camera on a rock and snapped a photo of ten radiant faces against a backdrop of splendor.

I didn't want to come down from that mountaintop. Like Peter on the Mount of Transfiguration, I wanted to build a few booths and camp out for a while in the glory of the moment.

Not long ago, I found that prized photograph of that special moment, and I realized that seven of the ten people in it had moved away from our area! Though Spike and I are still members of the same church, the church itself has undergone many changes. We have a new pastor. The membership has shifted and changed. There are new ministries, new hymns and choruses, new ways of doing things. It's still a wonderful church, but it's very different.

We could take a picture of that treasured moment in time and put it in a frame and hold on to it. But as much as I would like to, there was no way to frame and hold on to the moment itself. God wanted to give us all a new picture, a new vision, a new direction.

And now, in retrospect, I can see that I would not have wanted to miss his new vision. If I had dug my heels in and stayed focused on that old photograph, it would have faded and curled around the edges. My spiritual life would have grown stale and musty.

God was not finished with any of us. That's why we had to come down from the mountain and go on.

FOLLOW ME

When Jesus called to the men and women of the world he walked through, he was calling them to get unstuck. He was calling them to break loose from the safe and the predictable and the familiar. He offered no road maps, no guarantees given. He simply said, "Follow me!"

Some, like Peter and Andrew and Matthew, did just that. They followed. They left their jobs and their families and their home towns. They walked off from all that was familiar and dear.

Others, like the rich young ruler, turned their backs on Jesus and walked sadly away from him and his kingdom because their lives were so deeply lodged in the good things of this world that they couldn't risk the change.

In my journey so far, I've been cast in both roles. There have been times when I've followed. And there have been times when I've hung back, too afraid to let go, too terrified of the change. And from doing it both ways, I've discovered something important.

The times I've hung back and refused to change, I've found myself bogged down in a stagnant, lifeless pond, cut off from "the living water" of God's Spirit. The times I've followed, I've found myself swimming in the cool, exhilarating waters of God's abundant mercy. Sometimes the currents have been swift and challenging; sometimes I've gotten cold or tired or uncomfortable. But I've experienced the excitement of being "unstuck." And I've known the joy of moving on with him!

True confession time. For years, I resisted moving to the country. For years after I heard God calling and felt him nudging us to do it, I held back. I put my spiritual brakes on and spent all kinds of energy inventing creative rationales for why we should stay in town. I'm ashamed even to see that in writing, but it's true.

I was clinging to my possessions, to my neighborhood, to my own specifications and requirements for the kind of lifestyle that I felt I needed in order to be safe and comfortable. And God didn't force me to move. He just let me experience what it feels like to be out of the center of his will.

During those years, I began to get the feeling that my life was on hold. I was sitting there waiting for God to pick up the phone, but I was not hearing much from him. And though I was still praying and progressing by inches in some other areas of my life, nothing much was taking place overall.

"What's wrong, God," I would ask. "Where are you? Tell me what to do." But he had already told me what to do, and I just wasn't doing it!

Finally deciding to move has been like uncorking the stopper in a bottle for me. It has shaken things loose. It has gotten our lives back into action. Almost from the moment we put the "For Sale" sign in front of our house in town, we could feel our lives beginning to flow again.

As we get more and more acclimated to this new setting, Spike and I are beginning to see some of the reasons he wanted us to move. There's a new freedom here for us to rest, and a freedom to do more things together. New people and ideas and interests are pushing back the boundaries of our world. And although the move has felt uncomfortable and, yes, even traumatic at times, we cannot deny that it has also been life-giving.

Looking back on my reluctance to step out and follow what God was calling me to do, I can see now just how foolish it was. For me, clinging to my own stubborn plans when God was trying to move me into his new plan was like continuing to eat stale, rotting leftovers out of the refrigerator when a beautiful, abundant banquet had been set out for me in the next room. Or to use an old Bob Benson analogy, it was like clinging to my own stale, brown-bagged bologna sandwich at the church picnic when the best cook in town had invited me to sit on her home-made quilt and share her fried chicken, potato salad, fresh biscuits, and blueberry tarts!

NEVER SAY NEVER

Still I can't say I was surprised at the difficulties that our change posed for me. Our move was nothing I would ever have thought of doing on my own. In fact, I could never have even imagined myself living in a town of three hundred and fifty people!

Spike and I used to drive through little country towns like this one on our way to somewhere else, and I would frequently comment, "Who lives in these places? I could never live in a place like this. I'd go nuts."

Have you ever noticed that God is not really interested in pampering our preferences and prejudices? I am learning the hard way never to say never! I am learning that God knows better than I do what needs to be added to or subtracted from my life, and sometimes his idea of change involves the very thing that seems least desirable to me. God is going after our whole hearts. And when we draw a line in the dirt and say, "I could never do that," that is often the very place he'll call for a surrender.

God's hand of change almost always requires me to let go of something I have held dear or viewed as important or known for a fact. It calls me to let go of my own agenda, my own preferences and prejudices and ultimatums. It requires a yielding of my expectations and a welcoming of his reality. And it forces me to admit that I am not the expert on every subject, not even on my own life.

Mary and Martha had a very specific agenda as they waited for Jesus to arrive at their home in Bethany. They were waiting for him to heal their brother, Lazarus, who was seriously ill. So when Jesus was late in arriving and Lazarus died, Martha was not only grief-stricken; she was also more than a little bit annoyed with Jesus for not following her plan.

"If you had been here [like you were supposed to be], this would not have happened," she told him.

But all along Jesus had a different agenda. Martha and Mary were forced to let go of their own understanding of death and to trust Jesus to bring an incredible change into their lives.

"I believe that you are the Christ, the Son of God, who was to come into the world," Martha finally acknowledged. And it was at that point that he raised her brother from the dead.[6]

Peter, too, had to let go of a "know it all" attitude. If there was one thing that Peter understood, it was fishing. After all, he was a professional fisherman. So when Jesus suggested that he change his method of catching fish, Peter was somewhat indignant.

"Master," he said, in effect, "we've been working here all night long to catch fish. If there were any fish here, we would have caught them."

But when Peter was finally willing to stop being the authority on his own life, willing to try things Jesus' way, the result was a huge catch of fish, so large that it split Peter's nets.[7] And I can't help speculating that this was the Lord's way of preparing Peter to follow orders on faith as a future "fisher of men."

THE INCONVENIENT, THE UNEXPECTED—AND THE MIRACULOUS

God's changes in our lives frequently clash with our own ideas of what would be best. They are often inconvenient and unexpected and difficult to deal with.

A year or so back, my friend Nancy's life seemed nicely on course. At age forty-three, she was in the next-to-last semester of her Ph.D. program. Her children were progressing into adulthood. Her marriage was a happy one. Life was good.

When Nancy began to notice some changes in her body, her first thought was, "Oh, so this is 'the change of life' I've heard so much about." Little did she know just what a change of life it would be! Nine months later, little Patrick was born. Nancy's well-ordered life has suddenly been filled with cribs and bibs and midnight feedings! But in the midst of the chaos, Nancy and Don are discovering joy in one of God's unexpected miracles.

Seeing Nancy and Don with little Patrick, I can't help thinking of how Abraham and Sarah must have felt when little Isaac finally came along after all those years of waiting. Certainly, he was wanted. But how convenient is the arrival of any baby, much less one born to a couple of senior citizens?

Still, I'll bet Isaac kept Abraham and Sarah young in the same way that Patrick is keeping Nancy and Don young. Change keeps our spiritual joints from stiffening. Just as our bodies look and feel younger when we work at staying flexible, we remain young at heart when we stay mentally and spiritually flexible enough to welcome God's unexpected changes.

CHANGE ON TOP OF CHANGE

But sometimes change can throw a major curve to even the most flexible among us. When changes come in twos and threes, one after another, they can leave us floundering. Every change involves stress. And medical science has proved that multiple changes produce a kind of cumulative stress that, in turn, can cause anything from minor emotional upset to severe physical illness.

I really believe that's what happened to me this year. Before I had adjusted to one change, another one came along, then another. The next thing I knew, I was feeling down for the count. The "painful good-bye" was followed by "the move," which was followed by "the wedding" and "the birthday" and then "the empty nest." No wonder I've been reeling!

Just a few weeks ago, my physical workout provided me with a painful analogy to what happens when we experience too many significant changes in too short a time span. I had spent a Saturday night in town at my friend Signa's house and was jogging in her lovely, historic neighborhood the next morning before church. It was a beautiful day, and I was really enjoying running by row after row of renovated Victorian homes and gardens. What I didn't realize was that the roots of the huge oak trees in this old section of town have grown up under the sidewalks and broken through the concrete in places, causing buckling and bumps. Being unfamiliar with my route, I should have been watching my step instead of gaping at the scenery. Hitting one of those bumps head-on, I went sprawling face down on the sidewalk. Both elbows, both knees, and both hands were ripped open with painful brush burns.

Then, just four days later, before my wounds had even had a chance to heal, I fell again, this time on the sand road leading to our cabin. Not only were my injuries reopened, but they were now also full of sand. Ouch!

Soaking in a hot tub just after my second spill and feeling extremely sorry for myself, I realized that this was exactly what had been happening to me in the spiritual realm. Before I had even had time to heal from one change, here came another . . . and another. It was the cumulative affect that had really been getting me down.

Spike refers to the above analogy as "the parable of the scab." He says he especially likes to hear me tell it at the dinner table! But though not an appetizing tale, the "scab parable" does teach a pretty clear lesson. Change upon change has the effect of reopening wounds. Change upon change equals stress upon stress, for when changes happen in close proximity to one another, they can add high levels of unhealthy stress to our lives. (This is true of even the most positive changes, such as an eagerly anticipated move, a longed-for job promotion, or a new baby.) We need to be aware of the danger to our bodies and emotions and to give God the time and space he needs to heal us when changes mount up.

UNCHANGEABLE THINGS

One of the most healing things I can dwell on, in the thick of a lot of change, is the unchanging quality of God's love, the unchanging quality of his coming kingdom. There's a kind of balm in the words, "Jesus Christ is the same yesterday, today, and forever." Unlike all the fads and the crazes and the political regimes that surround us, he is and was and will be the same.

And I just have to believe that God is using the changes in my life today to chisel away all the temporary, earthly stuff about me so that he can remake me to eternal proportions, in the image of the Eternal One. So although right now I'm living day to day in what sometimes seems to be a world of turmoil and losses and good-byes, it's so good to know that I am on my way to a place where there will be no more death or tears or separations—ever.

When Spike's precious mom, Marjorie, was dying after a massive heart attack, all of us (her children) were allowed to be with her in the intensive care unit. Being there during the last hours of her life was one of the most faith-building experiences I have ever had. Even though her body was dying, we could almost see her spirit growing stronger and stronger right there in that hospital room.

Even with an oxygen tube in her mouth, drifting in and out of consciousness, she called out the chapters and verse numbers of the scriptures she wanted to hear. Dutifully, we looked them up and read them aloud to her, amazed at her knowledge of where to find the comfort she needed in the Word of God.

This is the verse which especially stands out in my memory:

All this is indeed working out for your benefit. . . . This is the reason why we never lose heart. The outward man does indeed suffer wear and tear, but every day the inward man receives fresh strength.

126

These little troubles (which are really so transitory) are winning for us a permanent, glorious and solid reward out of all proportion to our pain. For we are looking all the time not at the visible things but at the invisible. The visible things are transitory: it is the invisible things that are really permanent. We know, for instance, that if our earthly dwelling were taken down, like a tent, we have a permanent house in Heaven, made, not by man, but by God.[8]

Sitting there at the bedside of my brave little friend, my mother-in-law, I knew I was watching the most important metamorphosis of her life. Marjorie was being changed right before our eyes from someone earthbound to someone heavenly. Her earthly tent was being taken down, and she was moving into a permanent house that will never change. We knew that as she closed her eyes for the last time, they were fixed steadfastly not on the visible and transitory things of this life, but on the invisible, unchangeable, yesterday-today-and-forever things she'll never have to let go of.

These are the unchangeable things that you and I are being prepared for as we deal with all the changes in our everyday lives. We are being led from glory to glory, through a maze of sometimes unexpected, sometimes inconvenient, sometimes painful changes in preparation for a changeless kingdom where his love will reign forever.

And knowing about that unchangeable kingdom is a real boon when the changes in this world get us down. Dwelling on the unchangeable things makes the changes less traumatic when they come along. Recognizing God's purposes in our shifting circumstances opens us up to fully experience the inevitable and ongoing parade of changes we call life.

I consider that our present sufferings
are not worth comparing
with the glory that will be revealed in us.
The creation waits in eager expectation
for the sons of God to be revealed.
For the creation was subjected to frustration,
not by its own choice, but by the will
of the one who subjected it,
in hope that the creation itself
will be liberated from its bondage to decay and
brought into the glorious freedom of the children of God.

ROMANS 8:18–20 NIV

In the beginning, O Lord,
you laid the foundations of the earth,
and the heavens are the work of your hands.
They will perish, but you remain;
they will all wear out like a garment.
You will roll them up like a robe;
like a garment they will be changed.
But you remain the same,
and your years will never end.

HEBREWS 1:10–12 NIV

Celebrate Change

Picture your "comfort zone" as a warm, comfortable cardboard
box in which you feel totally protected and secure.
Imagine that strong, loving hands have set your
cardboard box on a sunny beach where the waves of God's love
are beginning to lap up and dissolve it.
Outside the dissolving box you can hear the voice of Jesus
calling you to follow him into a new adventure.
Gradually your cardboard walls soften and collapse.
You can feel the sun on your body. You look up into
the face of Jesus and see the love in his eyes.
You stretch slowly and stand up. Are you ready to follow?

Now give some time and thought to the following questions:
(1) What is your cardboard box? Is it a location,
the respect of certain people, a certain amount
in your savings account? (2) Whose hands are moving you
into a place of change? (3) To what adventure do you think
the Lord might be calling you? (4) What changes must be made
in order for you to follow him? [9]

*O Father, thank you for loving me just as I am. But thank you,
also, for loving me too much to leave me there.
Help me shake loose from my own selfish agenda,
my own personal preferences and prejudices. Help me let down
the barriers I've built between myself and your will for me.
Help me welcome as friends those sometimes inconvenient,
uncomfortable, and unexpected changes
you bring into my life. Give me courage to break out
of my comfort zone and follow you. Change me, Lord, from glory to
glory as you prepare me for your beautiful,
unchanging kingdom that is to come.*

AMEN

NINE

The Tale of the Orphan Prince

Claire's chapter about where we really belong

You gave me time
when no one gave me time of day,
you looked deep inside
while the rest of the world looked away,
you smiled at me
when there were just frowns everywhere—
you gave me love when nobody gave me a prayer.
And that's why I call you "Savior";
that's why I call you "Friend."
You touched my heart, you touched my soul,
and helped me start all over again.
And that's why I love you, Jesus;
that's why I'll always care:
You gave me love when nobody gave me a prayer.

You gave me laughter
after I cried all my tears,
you heard my dreams
when the rest of the world closed its ears,
I looked in your eyes,
and I saw the tenderness there—
You gave me love when nobody gave me a prayer.

And that's why I call you "Savior";
that's why I call you "Friend."
You touched my heart, you touched my soul,
and helped me start all over again.
And that's why I love you, Jesus.
that's why I'll always care:
You gave me love when nobody gave me a prayer.

CLAIRE CLONINGER AND ARCHIE P. JORDAN[1]

*M*y mama says she just loves the Bible because it's so full of quotations. (Actually, I think Mark Twain or somebody slightly more famous than Mama said it first.) But I love the Bible for its stories. It is full of amazing, heart-wrenching, life-changing stories, every one of them true.

There's the one about the man who gets swallowed by a large fish and is spit out on the exact beach he's been trying to avoid. Or there's the one about the guy who smites all these other guys with the jawbone of a donkey, but later gets his hair cut off and turns into a temporary wimp till his hair grows back and he pulls down a temple on the heads of everybody who ever teased him. Or what about the really old couple who laugh when they get the message that they're going to have a baby, and then, years later, when lo and behold they really do have one, actually name the little boy "Laughter"? Then there's the one about the guy who builds a mammoth boat in the middle of a desert because God tells him a storm is coming, which it does, so he gets all these animals aboard and floats around with them for about a month and a half while absolutely everybody apart from his immediate family sinks and drowns. And that's just for starters!

These stories have it all over fairy tales for my money. If some of the endings fall a bit short of happily ever after, that's mainly because they are more than just true; they are also alive![2] Reading them, you realize that people haven't changed all that much, and that God hasn't changed a bit. We're still blowing it, still needing him. And he's still calling us, drawing us, healing and forgiving us, even though we don't deserve it.

Some of the stories in the Bible are extremely well known. For example, most people (whether they believe a word of it or not) have probably heard the one about Noah's Ark. It's world famous.

But if you took a poll at the corner MacDonald's during lunch today, how many people do you think would have heard the one about the orphan prince, Mephibosheth? You probably couldn't even find one person in fifty who could *pronounce* Mephibosheth. Admit it. You probably can't pronounce Mephibosheth either.

But this little prince's story is a truly great one. For me, it paints a vivid and colorful picture of God's love for us, his children, in a way that nothing else ever has. That's why I want to share it with you now, in my own way, as something of a spiritual fairy tale.

THE ORPHAN PRINCE[3]

Once upon a time, in a tiny kingdom faraway, there lived a powerful king by the name of Saul. King Saul lived a life of wealth and plenty in the castle with his son, Jonathan, and his grandson, little Prince Mephibosheth.

All the people of the land loved Saul and Jonathan and Mephibosheth. But even more than they loved the royal family, the people loved Jonathan's best friend, David.

Long ago, when David had been just a boy, he had saved his people by slaying a wicked giant who was tormenting the tiny kingdom. But now David had grown up. He was strong and brave and handsome. It was said by many that he was the bravest knight in all of the tiny kingdom. Some even said David would someday take Saul's place as king.

Now, it happened that the tiny kingdom went to war with a neighboring land. King Saul, his son Jonathan, and Jonathan's friend David all strapped on their armor and rode bravely into battle with the other knights of the kingdom. They left little Prince Mephibosheth at home in the castle with his nursemaid, a kind and resourceful old woman who dearly loved the boy.

Every day King Saul and his knights would fight valiantly for the cause of the tiny kingdom. And every day a messenger would bring news of the battle to the castle where little Prince Mephibosheth and his nursemaid were waiting.

For many days the news was good, and for many days the nursemaid and the little prince felt safe in the castle. Then one day the messenger arrived with tears in his eyes, for the news from the battlefield that day was very sad, indeed.

"You must flee with the child," said the messenger to the nursemaid, "For this day both his grandfather, King Saul, and his father, Sir Jonathan, have been felled in battle. Who can know what fate will befall the little prince when a new king comes to power. Go at once without delay!"

Hastily the poor, frightened nursemaid gathered little Mephibosheth's belongings and prepared to flee the castle, carrying the little prince in her arms. But in her frenzy, she accidentally dropped the child on the hard, stone floor of the castle, badly injuring both of his legs.

How the nursemaid prayed that the child had not been seriously injured. But alas! Poor little Mephibosheth, son of Jonathan, grandson of Saul had been severely crippled. The orphan prince would always walk with a limp.

Now, there was a man named Makir who lived in the land of Lo Debar, just outside the boundaries of the tiny kingdom. It was to Makir's home that the nursemaid took the little prince, and there they stayed in hiding for fear of their lives.

Meanwhile, back in the tiny kingdom, it was decided that the brave knight, Sir David, should ascend the throne and succeed King Saul, who had fallen in battle. And so David became ruler of the tiny kingdom.

What a wise and fearless king he was! He led his people to many victories and accomplished great things in the land. He added to his country's wealth and achieved for his people great stature in the eyes of other kings and nations.

David should have been happy. He had everything anyone could desire: wealth and power and fame and the love of his people. And yet at times, when he was alone, the young king felt a great sadness in his heart. How he missed his friend, Jonathan!

"If only Jonathan were here to share all of this with me," David often thought.

Finally David hit upon an idea. He called together his counselors and advisors and put to them a question: "Is there anyone still left of the house of Saul to whom I can show kindness for my friend Jonathan's sake?"

"Well, your majesty," answered one of his wisest advisors, "An old man named Ziba, who was once a servant in the court of Saul, sits every day by the gates of the city reminiscing about the days when Saul was king. Perhaps he can answer your question. Shall I summon him to you, your majesty?"

"Yes," David answered excitedly. "Bring Ziba here to me at once."

The king's advisor returned shortly, bringing with him a wrinkled and ragged old man who trembled in fear at the thought of being brought before the throne of the new king. He was well aware that it was the custom for a new king to destroy or exile all who had been loyal to the former ruler.

Silence fell over the court as the old fellow at last stood before the throne. King David cleared his throat.

"Are you Ziba," he asked.

"Y-y-yes, your majesty, sire," the old man creaked. "I am Ziba, your servant."

"Well, can you tell me, Ziba," King David continued, "if there is anyone left of the household of Saul?"

The old man hesitated, still trembling.

"I wish them no harm," the new king added kindly. "I wish, rather, to show kindness to someone of Saul's household, for Jonathan was my dearest friend in all the world."

The old man's expression softened.

"Then I will tell you, sire," he answered. "There is someone—someone very close, in fact, to your friend Jonathan. Jonathan's son, Prince Mephibosheth, now lives in hiding with his nursemaid in the land of Lo Debar."

"Mephibosheth? Safe in Lo Debar? Oh, thank God!" King David exclaimed. "Please, go now and bring him here to me. And hurry back!"

And so the old man, Ziba, journeyed to Lo Debar, to the house of Makir, to bring back with him Prince Mephibosheth.

David's heart was brimming with excitement as he awaited the arrival of Jonathan's son. Years had passed since he had seen the boy. How had he changed? David wondered. Would he look like Jonathan? Would he be excited to return to his homeland after all this time in hiding? Or would he be frightened at being summoned before the new king?

Finally, after three long days, the doors to the great hall were thrown open, and the sound of a trumpet rang out.

"Mephibosheth, son of Jonathan, is here, your majesty," announced a loud and droning voice.

Through the massive, ornate doors of the tall-ceilinged hall hobbled a slender youth in clean but shabby clothes, leaning on a crude, wooden crutch. Behind him at a respectfully protective distance followed his kindly nursemaid, who was a very old woman by now. The young man had handsome features and a mane of thick, dark curls. His huge eyes were filled with fear.

"Come closer," said King David, marveling. How like Jonathan he was!

Slowly and laboriously, Mephibosheth made his way across the hard stone floors—the very same floors upon which he had been dropped years before. Finally he stood as erectly and as bravely as he could before the large, impressive throne—the very same throne upon which his grandfather had once sat.

"You are Mephibosheth?" King David asked.

"I am," replied the youth in as steady a voice as he could muster.

"Don't be afraid," the king said kindly. "I was your father's friend. Indeed, I am your friend. I have never intended you anything but kindness, Mephibosheth, but I had no idea where you had gone. What has your life been like since you left this castle? Where have you been? Please, tell me your story."

"The day my father and grandfather were killed, when I was only five, my nursemaid was advised to take me into hiding. We were told that our lives would be in danger, no matter who the next king might be, so she did as she was told. In her haste to depart, she dropped me, and it was then that I was crippled. We have been living in Lo Debar in the home of a friend for all these years, your majesty. We have never known whether it was safe to return to the kingdom of our birth, although we have often longed to."

Tears filled the good king's eyes, and compassion for the child of his friend flooded his heart.

"Why have you brought me here, my Lord?" the young man asked hesitantly.

"I wish to show you kindness, Mephibosheth, for the sake of your father, Jonathan. I wish to share with you all that I would certainly have shared with him had he lived. I wish to restore to you all that would have been yours by right had he not been taken from you. I wish to return to you all of the land, all of the possessions, all of the honor that once belonged to your grandfather, Saul. And I want you to come here to live with me. I want you always to eat at my table with my family."

Mephibosheth stood astonished and unable to speak. He lowered his eyes and shook his head as if to wake himself from a dream far too lovely to be real.

"Why are you so kind, my Lord? Why do you bother with someone who can do nothing to repay you?"

"Because Jonathan was my friend, you are my friend," David answered softly. "Because you were his son, you shall be my son. Do you understand?"

Mephibosheth nodded slowly, and for the first time since he had entered the castle a smile spread across his face, erasing the fear and tension from his dark eyes.

Then, with a wave of his hand, the king summoned Ziba once more. The weather-beaten old fellow, moved by the scene he had just witnessed, shuffled forward eagerly to await whatever instructions the king might have to give.

"Ziba," King David said with a note of authority in his voice, "I have given your master's grandson everything that once belonged to Saul and his family. Now I wish for you and your family to return to him and serve him exactly as you would have served his grandfather. You and your sons are to farm the land for him and bring in the crops, so that your master's grandson may be provided for. And you will no longer sit by the gate remembering days of old, but you will once more maintain a position of importance with the royal family. For Mephibosheth, the son of Jonathan, the grandson of Saul, shall now be my own son. And he will always eat at my table."

And so it came to pass that Mephibosheth, the orphan prince who was crippled in both legs, came to live at the castle with King David and was regarded as a prince once more among the subjects of the tiny kingdom. He grew strong and healthy and unafraid, and he came to depend on King David as the father he had lost.

And Ziba and his family farmed his fields, and brought in his crops, and served Mephibosheth as they had served his grandfather, Saul. But Mephibosheth always ate at the king's own table.

THE END

THE STORY OF EVERY BELIEVER

I believe the reason I love the story of the orphan prince so much is that it is the story of every believer. All of us were created to be children in the household of the King of kings. Yet all of us have been stripped of that birthright on the battlefield of sin. We've all been wounded and crippled and orphaned by this world and its fallenness.

And in the aftermath of the battle, all of us have found ourselves in hiding, pulling the filthy rags of our shame about us. Knowing in our heart of hearts that we were made for something better, we somehow have been unable to find our way back home.

Then one day, incredibly, we are called—summoned before the great King himself. We come with our heads bowed and our knees trembling, knowing we are unworthy to stand before him, yet mysteriously drawn into his presence.

Then, tenderly, he speaks our name, and we hear the kindness in his voice. Timidly we lift our eyes, and we see the mercy in his face. We listen in amazement to his words of healing and reconciliation, and we feel flooded with an awesome sense of hope. We feel his open arms fold gently about us, and we know that our hearts are finally home.

Home—not because we deserve it or can ever hope to earn it, but because, out of love for the one who stands at his throne and intercedes for us, he delights to give us the Kingdom . . . for free. He restores to us all that was lost, and he adopts us as his very own precious children. What's more, he calls us to a celebration at his table, where we can share in the bread and the wine of this glorious new kingdom whose gates are now open to us.

MY STORY, TOO

I love this story for very personal reasons, too. I love it because I know it is my own personal story.

I was certainly "in a far country" when I was called before the king. I had been "crippled" in my efforts to escape his rule in my life, and I was living as a spiritual refugee far away from him. He had sent lots of "messengers" and "servants" over the years to fetch me out of my various "hiding places," but I had stubbornly refused to be rescued.

Then, on a January night in 1977, I was able to see that my life was a mess without him. My own answers were frail and empty. My own ego, which had been on the throne of my life, was an insatiable despot. Finally, desperate enough and unhappy enough to know my need of the good King, I came out of hiding. Very much like a crippled orphan child, I dusted off my old Bible and "limped" into his presence. Feeling more than a little threadbare, I hobbled before his throne. Trembling and not quite sure what to expect, I looked into his face.

The mercy I found there I will never forget. The grace and love that was waiting for me in my Father's arms has rewritten the story of my life. Since that night, I have lived in his castle, eaten at his table, and known what it means to be a child of his kingdom.

I pray that, in some way or another, the story of the orphan prince is your story, too. If it is not yet, it is most certainly meant to be.

God, the good King, is waiting to welcome you as his child to your place in his kingdom—a place of safety and peace and privilege that was purchased for you by Jesus Christ. He is waiting to give you your spiritual inheritance—life, hope, joy, even eternity.

Your place is set at his table.

He's restlessly watching the road for the first sight of you in the distance.

He's eagerly listening at the door for your footstep.

Isn't it time you went on home?

But while he was still a long way off,
his father saw him and was filled with compassion for him;
he ran to his son, threw his arms around him and kissed him.
The son said to him, "Father, I have sinned
against heaven and against you.
I am no longer worthy to be called your son."
But the father said to his servants,
"Quick! Bring the best robe and put it on him.
Put a ring on his finger and sandals on his feet.
Bring the fattened calf and kill it.
Let's have a feast and celebrate.
For this son of mine was dead and is alive again;
he was lost and is found."

LUKE 15:20–23 NIV

Celebrate Being God's Child

If you have never given your life to Jesus, I encourage you
to take that step today. It's the most important
and life-changing decision you will ever make!
Tell him that you need his forgiveness, his mercy,
and his touch of new life. Come into his courts
with joy and abandon. Invite him to reign in your life.
There is no greater adventure in this world
than living as a child of the King!

If you do know what it's like to live as God's child,
write out a "fairy tale" parable of your spiritual journey.
Were you a scullery maid who was adopted by the King?
Were you under a spell until the Prince of Peace
came into your life? Describe your journey beginning with
"once upon a time" and ending with his promise of eternity.

❧

*Lord Jesus, I thank you for showing me your heart of mercy.
Thank you for continuing to seek me out
when I was in hiding. Thank you for constantly drawing me
back home to you, where I may dwell in your house
and always eat at your table. Forgive me for the sins
which have kept me from living as a child of your Kingdom.
I want you to reign in my heart and in my life.
I want you to be in control, to lead me and to guide me
in every large and small decision. I give you my life,
and I proclaim you as my King!*

AMEN

TEN

Someday My Prince Will Come

Karla's postscript about why it's going to be okay after all

The sink in the kitchen's dripping;
I think that we've sprung a leak.
It's time to buy some school supplies,
but cash is sure short this week.

My mother-in-law called Friday;
Dad's not doing all that well.
The doctors say it could go either way—
with these things you can never tell.

And right about now,
I could use some glory.
Right about now,
I sure need some grace.
Right about now,
I wish you could sit down at this table,
and I could see you face to face.
I wish I could pour you some coffee.
I wish that we could spend an hour.
Lord, I could sure use some glory
right about now.

KARLA WORLEY[1]

*S*o . . . *now you know.*

Now you know why you feel that vague sense of unrest, even though you have a good life and things are fine.

Now you know why, every now and then, you wonder, "Is this it? Is this as good as it gets?"

Now you know why so many of us have midlife crises and suddenly ask ourselves, "What have I really done with my life?"

Now you know why you have found yourself elbow deep in suds at the kitchen sink, wondering when someone's going to show up and pronounce you the princess that you are.

Now you know why you don't always feel like you fit in.

It's because you don't.

It's because you really are a child of a King, and this place is not your kingdom or your castle.

The old gospel song says it best:

> This world is not my home,
> I'm just a-passin' through.

Like Mephibosheth, you are an orphan here, an heir in hiding.

THE LOST KENNEDYS

I was in elementary school when President John F. Kennedy and his brother, Robert Kennedy were assassinated. My friends and I were all fascinated with these young leaders, with their glamorous families and their tragic lives. And I was especially captivated by the drama of Ethel Kennedy, Bobby's young widow, left alone with all those handsome children. I cut their pictures out of *Life* magazine. I even developed a secret crush on Bobby, Jr. I daydreamed about marrying him and helping his family not to be so sad.

I recently discovered that my friend Cindy also dreamed about the Kennedys when she was growing up. They seemed so dramatic, so much bigger than life, so . . . royal. Cindy, whose own father died when she was young, often felt sad and lonely, and so she imagined that she was really a Kennedy who'd somehow gotten separated at birth. She daydreamed that she would soon be discovered for the true blue-blood that she was and restored to her big, boisterous, romantically grand family.

Now, whenever we're feeling down or stressed out, Cindy and I tease each other about being the lost Kennedys. Just wait, we say; one day old Ted himself is going to show up on our doorstep and whisk us away to Hyannis Port to play football on the lawn.

I think that most of us have that sense of entitlement deep within us—that feeling that we should somehow be more than we are. That's why we're so fascinated with "royal moments" such as inaugurations and weddings. That's why we keep sending in our sweepstakes entries. That's why we watch the Miss America Pageant year after year. We love to see an average American girl turn into a princess right before our eyes.

When I was little, I would watch on those Saturday nights every year, in my jammies with my hair in pink sponge rollers, all set for Sunday school the next morning. I'd watch the pageant on the little black and white TV upstairs, in the dark, all by myself, so I could cry and nobody would see. The minute Burt Parks started singing "There She Is . . . ," I'd flip off the set and jump into bed, pretending to be asleep. I could hear my dad switch off the big TV down in the living room, turn off the lights, and slowly climb the stairs. He'd stop at the top, by the door to my room, and say softly into the darkness, "You're *my* Miss America." And I'd lie there in the dark in my pink sponge rollers and cry all the more. Everybody needs to feel she's somebody's princess!

NEVER ENOUGH

That sense of entitlement is okay. It is a part of being created by God, in his image. It is part of the proof that we are indeed his heirs, his children.

But the Deceiver of this world distorts those feelings, as he does with so many of the good things God created in us. (That's the way Satan works, taking what is natural and good about us and twisting it until it is sick and destructive.) He whispers in our ear, "You deserve more," until we are never satisfied. Nothing is ever enough.

Adam and Eve had it all—they lived in Paradise! They had their own little kingdom, hand-created, and the two of them reigned as king and queen over everything—everything, that is, except for that one tree. So Satan knew the spot to strike.

"He's not giving you everything," the snake whispered. "You deserve to have it all." Even Paradise was not enough.

We've all suffered with it since that day—that voice, the voice of the Deceiver, whispering inside us, even in the best moments, "This is not enough." That voice leads us into all kinds of quests for more—more money, more power, more recognition, more knowledge, more turn-ons, more fun, more freedom—anything to fill that void within that echoes, "Something is missing."

IS THAT ALL THERE IS?

In an article in the September 1992 issue of *Forbes* magazine, entitled "Why We Feel So Bad When We Have It So Good," author and White House speechwriter Peggy Noonan writes:

> Somewhere in the Seventies, or the Sixties, we started expecting to be happy, and changed our lives (left town, left families, switched jobs) if we were not. And society strained and cracked in the storm.
>
> I think we have lost the old knowledge that happiness is over-rated—that, in a way, life is overrated. We have lost, somehow , a sense of mystery—about us, our purpose, our meaning, our role. Our ancestors believed in two worlds, and understood this to be the solitary, poor, nasty, brutish and short one. We are the first genera-tions of man that actually expected to find happiness here on earth, and our search for it has caused such—unhappiness. The reason: If you do not believe in another, higher world, if you believe only in the flat material world around you, if you believe that this is your only chance at happiness—if that is what you believe, then you are not disappointed when the world does not give you a good measure of its riches, you are despairing.[2]

Despair haunts us, like a shadow at the edge of our mostly sunny lives. We run from it. We work too much, eat too much, drink too much, spend too much, watch too much TV. We do drugs, have affairs, get divorces to avoid despair. We push our children to overachieve, and we push ourselves, too. We fill our houses with things we don't need; we work overtime for power we don't have—the trappings of royalty. And yet we still feel estranged from something . . . something elusive.

We can't put our finger on it.

"More," we think. "There has to be more."

PROMISED GLORIES, PRESENT SORROWS

There is more.

There is a castle, and a throne. "In My Father's house are many mansions; if it were not so, I would have told you."[3]

There is a King and a kingdom. "Then the King will say to those on His right, 'Come, you who are blessed of My Father, inherit the kingdom prepared for you from the foundation of the world.'"[4]

And there is a crown. "When the Chief Shepherd appears, you will receive the unfading crown of glory."[5]

But these things are not in this world. "In this world, you will have trouble."[6] And our disappointment comes when we expect all that has been promised to come to us here and now.

The Crown Prince himself was an outcast here, a poor man. A carpenter, with calluses. A servant who washed feet, who served meals. A fisherman. Not a homeowner. Not an executive. Rarely in vogue. Often rejected.

As his fellow heirs, we should expect the same:

If the world hates you, you know that it has hated Me before it hated you. If you were of the world, the world would love its own; but because you are not of the world, but I chose you out of the world, therefore the world hates you. Remember the word that I said to you, "A slave is not greater than his master." If they persecuted Me, they will also persecute you.[7]

This is not the kingdom. Not yet.

"But take courage," Jesus assures us, "I have overcome the world."[8]

THE KING IS COMING

One day, the Bible tells us, the fanfare will sound. The King will come riding in. And we who belong to him will be given our crowns. We will reign with him. The glass slipper really will fit, and we'll have all the silver spoons we need.

And what do we do in the meantime?

Well, Cinderella had been to the ball. She had worn the dress, the crown, the slippers. She had ridden in the coach. She knew she was the one the prince had chosen. But the next morning, as always, she got up and served her stepmother's tea. She picked up her ugly stepsisters' ball gowns. She scrubbed the same floors and washed the same dishes. She dressed in the same old rags. And just think . . . all the time, she knew.

And now you know.

You know that this house, this furniture, these clothes, this body, this job, these chores . . . they're not all there is. Every now and then, in your child's laugh, your lover's touch, your friend's smile; in a sunset or a rainbow; when a neighbor comes through—every now and then you get a shining reminder of a kingdom that is beyond the here and now.

There is more than this life. That is our promise, our hope. And that is why we can sing.

Do you remember the Bible story about Paul and Silas, imprisoned in the town of Philippi for healing a girl in Jesus' name? God sent an earthquake to get them out of jail. But before that, beaten and chained, and stuffed in that musty dungeon, they were "praying and singing hymns of praise to God."9 Have you ever wondered just what they were singing that night? Maybe "I've Got a Mansion Just Over the Hillside"? Or perhaps, "The King Is Coming, the King Is Coming"? One thing is for certain: their sights were set on something far beyond their present circumstances.

And you and I, wherever we find ourselves at this moment—mopping floors, wiping noses, typing letters, closing deals, checking out groceries—can sing. Just close your eyes, smile to yourself, and hum, "Someday, My Prince Will Come."

Because, you know, he will.

Notes

Chapter 1

1. "Miracles Around Us," Lyric by Claire Cloninger/Karla Worley. © 1992 Word Music/ASCAP.
2. Phil. 4:11 LB.

Chapter 2

1. "Sweet Serenity," lyric/music by Claire Cloninger and Lynn Keesecker. © Word Music/ASCAP, 1990.

Chapter 3

1. Karla Worley, Seth's birth announcement, 26 April 1984.
2. 1 Cor. 11:24 NKJV.

Chapter 4

1. "I Love You For Free," words and music by Claire Cloninger and Jamie Harvill. © Word Music and Paths of Peace Music, 1991.
2. "Sure Beats Hell," Lyric by Claire Cloninger, Melody by Tommy Greer, © Word Music, 1991.
3. These are my own words; the story is old as the hills!
4. See John 8:3–11.
5. See Matt. 19:13–15, Mark 10:13–16, Luke 18:15–17.
6. See Luke 19:1–9.
7. See Matt. 8:28–33, Mark 5:2–6, Luke 8:27–36.
8. Brennan Manning, *The Ragamuffin Gospel: Good News for the Bedraggled, Beat-Up, and Burnt Out* (Portland, OR: Multnomah, 1990), 11–12.
9. Quoted in Tim Hansel, *Holy Sweat* (Waco, TX: Word, 1987), 13.
10. John 15:15 NIV.

Chapter 5

1. "Tell Him So," Lyric/Music by Tim Sheppard/Karla Worley. © 1990 Housewife Music/ASCAP; Diadem Sky/ASCAP; Tim Sheppard Music/ASCAP.
2. Eccles. 3:1 NASB.
3. Jer. 29:11 NASB.
4. Prov. 3:5 NASB.
5. Phil. 4:19 NASB.

Chapter 6

1. "What Would I Do Without You?" Lyric by Claire Cloninger © Word, Inc., 1991.
2. Calvin Miller, *If This Be Love* (San Francisco: Harper & Row, 1984), vi.
3. Eph. 3:21 PHILLIPS.

Chapter 7

1. "The Way We Praise Him," Lyric by Karla Worley/Music by Billy Crockett and Karla Worley. © 1990 Housewife Music/ASCAP; Diadem Sky/ASCAP; Radar Days Music/ASCAP.
2. Matt. 25:23 NKJV.
3. Mark 10:42–45 NASB.
4. Matt. 25:40 NKJV.
5. See John 21:15–19 NKJV.

Chapter 8

1. "The More Things Change," Lyric by Claire Cloninger/Music by Billy Smiley. © Word Music/Sparrow, 1986.
2. Taken from the Dave Barry 1992 desk calendar.
3. Anne Tyler, *Saint Maybe* (New York: Ivy Books, 1991), 349.
4. Sue Monk Kidd, *When the Heart Waits: Spiritual Direction for Life's Sacred Questions* (San Francisco: Harper and Row, 1990), 4.
5. Heb. 11:13–16, 1 Pet. 2:10–12.
6. John 11:1–43, paraphrased from the NIV.
7. Luke 5:1–11, paraphrased from the NIV.
8. 2 Cor. 4:15–18; 5:1 PHILLIPS.

9. I first heard this "cardboard box" exercise used in a teaching by Mickey Smith of Mobile.

Chapter 9

1. "You Gave Me Love," Lyric and melody by Claire Cloninger and Archie P. Jordan. © Word, Inc., 1979.

2. John 6:63.

3. Taken from 2 Samuel 4:4 and 9:1–13.

Chapter 10

1. "Right About Now," Lyric/Music by Karla Worley. © 1992 Word Music/ASCAP.

2. Peggy Noonan, "You'd Cry Too, If It Happened to You," *Forbes*, September 1992.

3. John 14:2 NKJV.

4. Matt. 25:34 NASB.

5. 1 Peter 5:4 NASB.

6. John 16:33 NIV.

7. John 15:18–20 NASB.

8. John 16:33 NASB.

9. Acts 16:25.